PU

INTRODUCIN

There are twelve boo
bursting with splendid stories about with the kind face and the very special gift of talking to animals and, for any child who can read well, these miraculously inventive, wise, kindly stories are just perfect for embarking on a long, satisfying read.

But what about younger children, who aren't such good readers? Their parents may never have time to read them the whole twelve books, so here is a chance to get to know the endearing Doctor before they are ready to tackle the longer books. *Introducing Doctor Dolittle* (first published by Jonathan Cape as *Doctor Dolittle: A Treasury*) is designed to give younger readers a window on the Dolittle world and introduce them to his chosen companions and pets, DAB-DAB the duck, JIP the dog, TOO-TOO the owl, POLYNESIA the parrot, and the rest.

They may learn here for the first time how the Doctor discovered it was possible to talk to the animals at all, how he acquired the strange two-headed African pushmipullyu, saved SOPHIE the seal from the circus, how he travelled to a legendary floating island and what detained him there, and many other fascinating stories – and if they don't at the same time learn to love Doctor Dolittle and long for more we shall be very surprised.

The stories are reproduced here in just the same words as Hugh Lofting originally used, and were chosen by his sister-in-law, Olga Fricker, who has been a lifelong admirer of his works, and is surely better qualified than most to make selections from them.

Hugh Lofting

INTRODUCING DOCTOR DOLITTLE

Compiled by Olga Fricker

PUFFIN BOOKS

Puffin Books, Penguin Books Ltd, Harmondsworth, Middlesex, England
Viking Penguin Inc., 40 West 23rd Street, New York, New York 10010, U.S.A
Penguin Books Australia Ltd, Ringwood, Victoria, Australia
Penguin Books Canada Ltd, 2801 John Street, Markham, Ontario, Canada L3R 1B4
Penguin Books (N.Z.) Ltd, 182–190 Wairau Road, Auckland 10, New Zealand

—

First published as *Doctor Dolittle: A Treasury* in the U.S.A. 1967
Published in Great Britain by Jonathan Cape 1968
Published as *Introducing Doctor Dolittle* in Puffin Books 1977
Reprinted 1980, 1985

—

—

Made and printed in Great Britain by
Richard Clay (The Chaucer Press) Ltd,
Bungay, Suffolk
Set in Intertype Pilgrim

CONTENTS

LIST OF ILLUSTRATIONS

LIST OF ILLUSTRATIONS

FOREWORD

THE treasure that Hugh Lofting left to the world began to take shape in the letters which, as a young Captain in the Irish Guards early in the First World War, he wrote to his two children, Colin and Elizabeth. It is not unusual for a soldier under the stress of war, and lonely for his family, to write letters home. What was unusual here is that these letters were stories about an English village doctor, created from the imagination and compassion of Hugh Lofting. The stories told how John Dolittle, M.D., loved animals and gave up his human practice to become a doctor to animals, certainly the best the world had ever known because he learned to speak and to understand animal-language. Hugh Lofting made drawings to send to his children with the 'letters', the same kind of drawings that later appeared in the published books. The first of these was *The Story of Doctor Dolittle*, which Jonathan Cape published in 1922, followed by eleven other Doctor Dolittle books in the ensuing years.

Introducing Doctor Dolittle is not a substitute for them. It is conceived to provide children with an introduction to the world of Doctor Dolittle, at a popular price, comprising material *just as Hugh Lofting wrote it*, including his own illustrations. Miss Olga Fricker, sister of the late Mrs Hugh Lofting and a lifelong Doctor Dolittle enthusiast, has compiled and organized the material from the original works. In making her selections she was guided by her judgement of which chapters of the twelve books would be most representative and most entertaining for the child coming to Doctor Dolittle for the first time. Readers of the books know that many of the chapters, while part of the whole, are complete incidents in themselves. *Introducing*

Doctor Dolittle is, therefore, in form quite similar to that of the original volumes. There is very little sense of 'separateness' from selection to selection, because Doctor Dolittle himself is always there, and the same animal characters appear and reappear throughout the selections.

Of special interest to collectors and children's-book bibliophiles is the fact that *Introducing Doctor Dolittle* includes twenty-six Hugh Lofting drawings never before published in book form, as well as many others taken from the original books. Mr Lofting drew many more illustrations than could be used in the books when published, and fortunately, they have been preserved.

It is hoped that this single volume will initially bring more children, possibly at an earlier age, to Doctor Dolittle than could the twelve separate books, and that *Introducing Doctor Dolittle* will serve as an invitation to the later, more leisurely delight of reading each of the original volumes.

THE

Story of

DOCTOR DOLITTLE

BEING THE
HISTORY OF HIS PECULIAR LIFE
AT HOME AND ASTONISHING ADVENTURES
IN FOREIGN PARTS. NEVER BEFORE PRINTED.

TOLD BY HUGH LOFTING ILLUSTRATED BY THE AUTHOR

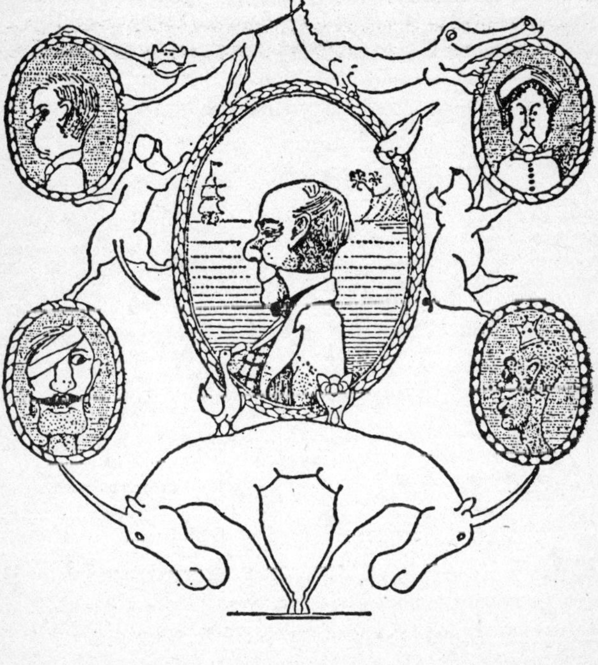

PUDDLEBY

ONCE upon a time, many years ago – when our grandfathers were little children – there was a doctor; and his name was Dolittle – John Dolittle, M.D. 'M.D.' means that he was a proper doctor and knew a whole lot.

He lived in a little town called Puddleby-on-the-Marsh. All the folks, young and old, knew him well by sight. And whenever he walked down the street in his high hat everyone would say, 'There goes the Doctor! – he's a clever man.' And the dogs and the children would all run up and follow behind him; and even the crows that lived in the church tower would caw and nod their heads.

The house he lived in, on the edge of the town, was quite small; but his garden was very large and had a wide lawn and stone seats and weeping-willows hanging over. His sister, Sarah Dolittle, was housekeeper for him; but the Doctor looked after the garden himself.

He was very fond of animals and kept many kinds of pets. Besides the goldfish in the pond at the bottom of his garden, he had rabbits in the pantry, white mice in his piano, a squirrel in the linen closet, and a hedgehog in the cellar. He had a cow with a calf too, and an old lame horse – twenty-five years of age – and chickens, and pigeons, and two lambs, and many other animals. But his favourite pets were Dab-Dab the duck, Jip the dog, Gub-Gub the baby pig, Polynesia the parrot, and the owl Too-Too.

His sister used to grumble about all these animals and said they made the house untidy. And one day when an old lady with rheumatism came to see the Doctor, she sat on the hedgehog who was sleeping on the sofa and never came to see him any more, but drove every Saturday all the way to Oxenthorpe, another town ten miles off, to see a different doctor.

Then his sister, Sarah Dolittle, came to him and said,

'John, how can you expect sick people to come and see you when you keep all these animals in the house? It's a fine doctor would have his parlour full of hedgehogs and mice! That's the fourth personage these animals have driven away. Squire Jenkins and the Parson say they wouldn't come near your house again – no matter how sick they are. We are getting poorer every day. If you go on like this, none of the best people will have you for a doctor.'

A little town called Puddleby-on-the-Marsh

'But I like the animals better than the "best people",' said the Doctor.

'You are ridiculous,' said his sister, and walked out of the room.

So, as time went on, the Doctor got more and more animals; and the people who came to see him got less and less, till at last he had no one left – except the Cat's-meat-Man, who didn't mind any kind of animals. But the Cat's-meat-Man wasn't very rich and he only got sick once a year – at Christmas-time, when he used to give the Doctor sixpence for a bottle of medicine.

Sixpence a year wasn't enough to live on – even in those days, long ago; and if the Doctor hadn't had some money saved up in his money-box, no one knows what would have happened.

And he kept on getting still more pets; and of course it cost a lot to feed them. And the money he had saved up grew littler and littler.

Then he sold his piano, and let the mice live in a bureau drawer. But the money he got for that too began to go, so he sold the brown suit he wore on Sundays and went on becoming poorer and poorer.

And now, when he walked down the street in his high hat, people would say to one another, 'There goes John Dolittle, M.D.! There was a time when he was the best-known doctor in the West Country. Look at him now – he hasn't any money and his stockings are full of holes!'

But the dogs and cats and the children still ran up and followed him through the town – the same as they had done when he was rich.

ANIMAL-LANGUAGE

It happened one day that the Doctor was sitting in his kitchen talking with the Cat's-meat-Man who had come to see him with a stomach-ache.

'Why don't you give up being a people's doctor, and be an animal-doctor?' asked the Cat's-meat-Man.

The parrot, Polynesia, was sitting in the window looking out at the rain and singing a sailor-song to herself. She stopped singing and started to listen.

'You see, Doctor,' the Cat's-meat-Man went on, 'you know all about animals – much more than what these here vets do. That book you wrote – about cats, why, it's wonderful! I can't read or write myself – or maybe *I'd* write some books. But my wife,

Theodosia, she's a scholar, she is. And she read your book to me. Well, it's wonderful – that's all can be said – wonderful. You might have been a cat yourself. You know the way they think. And listen: you can make a lot of money doctoring animals. Do you know that? You see, I'd send all the old women who had sick cats or dogs to you. And if they didn't get sick fast enough, I could put something in the meat I sell 'em to make 'em sick, see?'

'Oh, no,' said the Doctor quickly. 'You mustn't do that, that wouldn't be right.'

'Oh, I didn't mean real sick,' answered the Cat's-meat-Man. 'Just a little something to make them droopy-like was what I had reference to. But as you say, maybe it ain't quite fair on the animals. But they'll get sick anyway, because the old women always give 'em too much to eat. And look, all the farmers round about who had lame horses and weak lambs – they'd come. Be an animal-doctor.'

When the Cat's-meat-Man had gone the parrot flew off the window on to the Doctor's table and said:

'That's man's got sense. That's what you ought to do. Be an animal-doctor. Give the silly people up – if they haven't brains enough to see you're the best doctor in the world. Take care of animals instead – they'll soon find it out. Be an animal-doctor.'

'Oh, there are plenty of animal-doctors,' said John Dolittle, putting the flower-pots outside on the window-sill to get the rain.

'Yes, there *are* plenty,' said Polynesia. 'But none of them are any good at all. Now listen, Doctor, and I'll tell you something. Did you know that animals can talk?'

'I knew that parrots can talk,' said the Doctor.

'Oh, we parrots can talk in two languages – people's language and bird-language,' said Polynesia proudly. 'If I say, "Polly wants a cracker," you understand me. But hear this: *Ka-ka oi-ee, fee-fee?*'

'Good gracious!' cried the Doctor. 'What does that mean?'

'That means, "Is the porridge hot yet?" – in bird-language.'

'My! You don't say so!' said the Doctor. 'You never talked that way to me before.'

'What would have been the good?' said Polynesia, dusting some cracker-crumbs off her left wing. 'You wouldn't have understood me if I had.'

'Tell me some more,' said the Doctor, all excited; and he rushed over to the dresser-drawer and came back with the butcher's book and a pencil. 'Now don't go too fast – and I'll write it down. This is interesting – very interesting – something quite new. Give me the birds' A.B.C. first – slowly now.'

So that was the way the Doctor came to know that animals had a language of their own and could talk to one another. And all that afternoon, while it was raining, Polynesia sat on the kitchen table, giving him bird words to put down in the book.

At tea-time, when the dog, Jip, came in, the parrot said to the Doctor, 'See, *he's* talking to you.'

'Looks to me as though he were scratching his ear,' said the Doctor.

'But animals don't always speak with their mouths,' said the parrot in a high voice, raising her eyebrows. 'They talk with their ears, with their feet, with their tails – with everything. Sometimes they don't *want* to make a noise. Do you see now the way he's twitching up one side of his nose?'

'What's that mean?' asked the Doctor.

'That means, "Can't you see that it's stopped raining?"' Polynesia answered. 'He is asking you a question. Dogs nearly always use their noses for asking questions.'

After a while, with the parrot's help, the Doctor got to learn the language of the animals so well that he could talk to them himself and understand everything they said. Then he gave up being a people's doctor altogether.

As soon as the Cat's-meat-Man had told everyone that John Dolittle was going to become an animal-doctor, old ladies began to bring him their pet pugs and poodles who had eaten too much cake; and farmers came many miles to show him sick cows and sheep.

One day a plough horse was brought to him; and the poor thing was terribly glad to find a man who could talk in horse-language.

'You know, Doctor,' said the horse, 'that vet over the hill knows nothing at all. He has been treating me six weeks now – for spavins. What I need is *spectacles*. I am going blind in one eye. There's no reason why horses shouldn't wear glasses, the same as people. But that stupid man over the hill never even looked at my eyes. He kept on giving me big pills. I tried to tell him; but he couldn't understand a word of horse-language. What I need is spectacles.'

'Of course – of course,' said the Doctor. 'I'll get you some at once.'

'I would like a pair like yours,' said the horse, 'only green. They'll keep the sun out of my eyes while I'm ploughing the Fifty Acre Field.'

'Certainly,' said the Doctor. 'Green ones you shall have.'

'You know, the trouble is, sir,' said the plough horse as the Doctor opened the front door to let him out, 'the trouble is that *anybody* thinks he can doctor animals – just because the animals don't complain. As a matter of fact it takes a much cleverer man to be a really good animal-doctor than it does to be a people's doctor. My farmer's boy thinks he knows all about horses. I wish you could see him – his face is so fat he looks as though he has no eyes – and he has got as much brain as a potato-bug. He tried to put a mustard-plaster on me last week.'

'Where did he put it?' asked the Doctor.

'Oh, he didn't put it anywhere – on me,' said the horse. 'He only tried to. I kicked him into the duck-pond.'

'Well, well!' said the Doctor.

'I'm a pretty quiet creature as a rule,' said the horse, 'very patient with people – don't make much fuss. But it was bad enough to have that vet giving me the wrong medicine. And when that red-faced booby started to monkey with me, I just couldn't bear it any more.'

'Did you hurt the boy much?' asked the Doctor.

'Oh, no,' said the horse. 'I kicked him in the right place. The vet's looking after him now. When will my glasses be ready?'

'I'll have them for you next week,' said the Doctor. 'Come in again Tuesday. Good morning!'

Then John Dolittle got a fine, big pair of green spectacles; and the plough horse stopped going blind in one eye and could see as well as ever.

And soon it became a common sight to see farm-animals wearing glasses in the country round Puddleby; and a blind horse was a thing unknown.

And so, in a few years' time, every living thing for miles and miles got to know about John Dolittle, M.D. And the birds who flew to other countries in the winter told the animals in foreign

He could see as well as ever

lands of the wonderful doctor of Puddleby-on-the-Marsh, who could understand their talk and help them in their troubles. In this way he became famous among the animals all over the world; better known even than he had been among the folks of the West Country. And he was happy and liked his life very much.

One afternoon when the Doctor was busy writing in a book, Polynesia sat in the window – as she nearly always did – looking out at the leaves blowing about in the garden.

The Doctor looked up and said, 'How old are you, Polynesia? I know that parrots and elephants sometimes live to be very, very old.'

'I can never be quite sure of my age,' said Polynesia. 'It's either a hundred and eighty-three or a hundred and eighty-two. But I know that when I first came here from Africa, King Charles was still hiding in the oak-tree – because I saw him. He looked scared to death.'

MORE MONEY TROUBLES

AND soon now the Doctor began to make money again; and his sister, Sarah, bought a new dress and was happy.

Some of the animals who came to see him were so sick that they had to stay at the Doctor's house for a week. And when they were getting better they used to sit in chairs on the lawn.

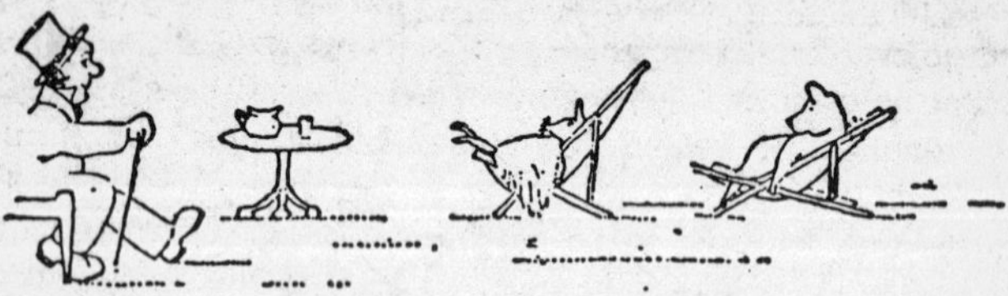

They used to sit in chairs on the lawn

And often, even after they got well, they did not want to go away – they liked the Doctor and his house so much. And he never had the heart to refuse them when they asked if they could stay with him. So in this way he went on getting more and more pets.

Once when he was sitting on his garden wall, smoking a pipe in the evening, an organ-grinder came round with a monkey on a string. The Doctor saw at once that the monkey's collar was too tight and that he was dirty and unhappy. So he took the monkey away from the organ-grinder, gave the man a shilling, and told him to go. The organ-grinder got awfully angry and said that he wanted to keep the monkey. But the Doctor told him that if he didn't go he would punch him on the nose. John Dolittle was a strong man, though he wasn't very tall. So the man went away saying rude things and the monkey stayed with Doctor Dolittle and had a good home. The other animals in the house called him 'Chee-Chee' – which is a common word in monkey-language, meaning 'ginger'.

And another time, when the circus came to Puddleby, the crocodile, who had a bad toothache, escaped at night and came into the Doctor's garden. The Doctor talked to him in crocodile-language and took him into the house and made his tooth better. But when the crocodile saw what a nice house it was – with all the different places for the different kinds of animals – he, too, wanted to live with the Doctor. He asked couldn't he sleep in the fish-pond at the bottom of the garden, if he promised not to eat the fish. When the circus-men came to take him back he got so wild and savage that he frightened them away. But to everyone in the house he was always as gentle as a kitten.

But now the old ladies grew afraid to send their lap-dogs to Doctor Dolittle because of the crocodile; and the farmers wouldn't believe that he would not eat the lambs and sick calves they brought to be cured. So the Doctor went to the crocodile and told him he must go back to the circus. But he wept such big tears, and begged so hard to be allowed to stay, that the Doctor hadn't the heart to turn him out.

So then the Doctor's sister came to him and said,

'John, you must send that creature away. Now the farmers and the old ladies are afraid to send their animals to you – just as we were beginning to be well off again. Now we shall be ruined entirely. This is the last straw. I will no longer be housekeeper for you if you don't send away that alligator.'

'It isn't an alligator,' said the Doctor, 'it's a crocodile.'

'I don't care what you call it,' said his sister. 'It's a nasty thing to find under the bed. I won't have it in the house.'

'But he has promised me,' the Doctor answered, 'that he will not bite anyone. He doesn't like the circus; and I haven't the money to send him back to Africa where he comes from. He minds his own business and on the whole is very well behaved. Don't be so fussy.'

'I tell you I *will not* have him around,' said Sarah. 'He eats the linoleum. If you don't send him away this minute I'll – I'll go and get married!'

'All right,' said the Doctor, 'go and get married. It can't be helped.' And he took his hat and went out into the garden.

So Sarah Dolittle packed her things and went off; and the Doctor was left alone with his animal family.

And very soon he was poorer than he had ever been before. With all these mouths to fill, and the house to look after, and no one to do the mending, and no money coming in to pay the butcher's bill, things began to look very difficult. But the Doctor didn't worry at all.

'Money is a nuisance,' he used to say. 'We'd all be much better off if it had never been invented. What does money matter, so long as we are happy?'

But Too-Too, the owl, who was good at arithmetic, figured out that there was only money enough left to last another week – if they each had one meal a day and no more.

Then the animals made a vegetable and flower stall outside the garden-gate and sold radishes and roses to the people that passed by along the road.

But still they didn't seem to make enough money to pay all the bills – and still the Doctor didn't worry.

He didn't even worry when Chee-Chee, the monkey, came to him panting and badly out of breath.

'Doctor!' he cried. 'I've just had a message from a cousin of mine in Africa. There is a terrible sickness among the monkeys out there. They are all catching it – and they are dying in hundreds.'

'Dear me!' said the Doctor. 'Then we shall just have to go to Africa.'

'But that takes money,' said Dab-Dab, who was always practical about such things.

'Well, well,' murmured the Doctor. 'Never mind. Perhaps if I go down to the seaside I shall be able to borrow a boat that will take us to Africa. I knew a seaman once who brought his baby to me with measles. Maybe he'll lend me his boat – the baby got well.'

So early the next morning the Doctor went down to the seashore. And when he came back he told the animals it was all right – the sailor was going to lend them the boat.

And the voyage began

The sailor even borrowed enough food for them to stock the ship for the journey, and the Doctor and his whole family went off to Africa.

Although the ship was wrecked in a bad storm on the coast of Africa, they all got ashore safely.

It didn't take Doctor Dolittle long to cure the monkeys of their sickness, and they were so grateful they wanted to give him a going-away present. They asked Chee-Chee what the Doctor would like.

'Why not give him a rare animal,' suggested Chee-Chee. 'He could then charge people to see it and never have to be without money again.'

And the chief of the monkeys asked:

'Have they an iguana over there?'

'Yes, there is one in the London Zoo,' replied Chee-Chee.

And another asked, 'Have they an okapi?'

But Chee-Chee said, 'Yes, in Belgium, where my organ-grinder took me five years ago, they have an okapi in a big city they call Antwerp.'

And another asked, 'Have they a pushmi-pullyu?'

Then Chee-Chee said, 'No. No white man has ever seen a pushmi-pullyu. Let us give him that.'

THE RAREST ANIMAL OF ALL

PUSHMI-PULLYUS are now extinct. That means there aren't any more. But long ago, when Doctor Dolittle was alive, there were some of them still left in the deepest jungle of Africa; and even then they were very scarce. They had no tail, but a head at each end, and sharp horns on each head. They were very shy and terribly hard to catch. The natives get most of their animals by sneaking up behind them while they are not looking. But you could not do this with the pushmi-pullyu, because, no matter which way you came towards him, he was always facing you. And besides, only one half of him slept at a time. The other head was always awake – and watching. This was why they were never caught and never seen in zoos. Though many of the greatest huntsmen and the cleverest menagerie-keepers spent years of their lives searching through the jungles in all weathers for pushmi-pullyus, not a single one had ever been caught. Even then, years ago, he was the only animal in the world with two heads.

Well, the monkeys set out hunting for this animal through the forest. And after they had gone a good many miles, one of them found peculiar footprints near the edge of a river; and they knew that a pushmi-pullyu must be very near the spot.

Then they went along the bank of the river a little way and they saw a place where the grass was high and thick; and they guessed that he was in there.

So they all joined hands and made a great circle round the high grass. The pushmi-pullyu heard them coming; and he tried hard to break through the ring of monkeys. But he couldn't do it. When he saw that it was no use trying to escape, he sat down and waited to see what they wanted.

They asked him if he would go with Doctor Dolittle and be put on show in the Land of the White Men.

But he shook both his heads hard and said, 'Certainly not!'

They explained to him that he would not be shut up in a menagerie but would just be looked at. They told him that the Doctor was a very kind man but hadn't any money; and people would pay to see a two-headed animal and the Doctor would get rich and could pay for the boat he had borrowed to come to Africa in.

But he answered, 'No. You know how shy I am – I hate being stared at.' And he almost began to cry.

Then for three days they tried to persuade him.

And at the end of the third day he said he would come with them and see what kind of a man the Doctor was, first.

So the monkeys travelled back with the pushmi-pullyu. And when they came to where the Doctor's little house of grass was, they knocked on the door.

The duck, who was packing the trunk, said, 'Come in!'

And Chee-Chee very proudly took the animal inside and showed him to the Doctor.

'What in the world is it?' asked John Dolittle, gazing at the strange creature.

'Lord save us!' cried the duck. 'How does it make up its mind?'

'It doesn't look to me as though it had any,' said Jip the dog.

'This, Doctor,' said Chee-Chee, 'is the pushmi-pullyu – the rarest animal of the African jungles, the only two-headed beast in the world! Take him home with you and your fortune's made. People will pay any money to see him.'

'But I don't want any money,' said the Doctor.

'Yes, you do,' said Dab-Dab the duck. 'Don't you remember how we had to pinch and scrape to pay the butcher's bill in Puddleby? And how are you going to get the sailor the new boat you spoke of – unless we have the money to buy it?'

'I was going to make him one,' said the Doctor.

'Lord save us!' cried the duck. 'How does it make up its mind?'

'Oh, do be sensible!' cried Dab-Dab. 'Where would you get all the wood and the nails to make one with? – And besides, what are we going to live on? We shall be poorer than ever when we get back. Chee-Chee's perfectly right: take the funny-looking thing along, do!'

'Well, perhaps there is something in what you say,' murmured the Doctor. 'It certainly would make a nice new kind of pet. But does the – er – what-do-you-call-it really want to go abroad?'

'Yes, I'll go,' said the pushmi-pullyu who saw at once, from the Doctor's face, that he was a man to be trusted. 'You have been so kind to the animals here – and the monkeys tell me that I am the only one who will do. But you must promise me that if I do not like it in the Land of the White Men you will send me back.'

'Why, certainly – of course, of course,' said the Doctor. 'Excuse me, surely you are related to the Deer Family, are you not?'

'Yes,' said the pushmi-pullyu, 'to the Abyssinian Gazelles and the Asiatic Chamois – on my mother's side. My father's great-grandfather was the last of the Unicorns.'

'Most interesting!' murmured the Doctor; and he took a book out of the trunk which Dab-Dab was packing and began turning the pages. 'Let us see if Buffon says anything – '

'I notice,' said the duck, 'that you only talk with one of your mouths. Can't the other head talk as well?'

'Oh, yes,' said the pushmi-pullyu. 'But I keep the other mouth for eating – mostly. In that way I can talk while I am eating without being rude. Our people have always been very polite.'

When the packing was finished and everything was ready to start, the monkeys gave a grand party for the Doctor, and all the animals of the jungle came. And they had pineapples and mangoes and honey and all sorts of good things to eat and drink.

After they had all finished eating, the Doctor got up and said,

'My friends: I am not clever at speaking long words after dinner, like some men; and I have just eaten many fruits and much honey. But I wish to tell you that I am very sad at leaving your beautiful country. Because I have things to do in the Land of the White Men, I must go. After I have gone, remember never to let the flies settle on your food before you eat it; and do not sleep on the ground when the rains are coming. I – er – er – I hope you will all live happily ever after.'

When the Doctor stopped speaking and sat down, all the monkeys clapped their hands a long time and said to one another, 'Let it be remembered always among our people that he sat and ate with us, here, under the trees. For surely he is the Greatest of Men!'

And the Grand Gorilla, who had the strength of seven horses

in his hairy arms, rolled a great rock up to the head of the table and said,

'This stone for all time shall mark the spot.'

And even to this day, in the heart of the jungle, that stone still is there. And monkey-mothers, passing through the forest with their families, still point down at it from the branches and whisper to their children, 'Sh! There it is – look – where the Good White Man sat and ate food with us in the Year of the Great Sickness!'

Then, when the party was over, the Doctor and his pets started out to go back to the seashore. And all the monkeys went with him as far as the edge of their country, carrying his trunk and bags, to see him off.

DOCTOR
DOLITTLE'S
CIRCUS
TOLD AND ILLUSTRATED BY
HUGH LOFTING

THE PUSHMI-PULLYU

THIS is the story of that part of Doctor Dolittle's adventures which came about through his joining and travelling with a circus. He had not planned in the beginning to follow this life for any considerable time. His intention had only been to take the pushmi-pullyu out on show long enough to make sufficient money to pay the sailor back for the boat which had been borrowed and wrecked on his way to Africa.

But a remark Too-Too had made was true: it was not so hard for John Dolittle to become rich – for indeed he was easily satisfied where money was concerned – but it was a very different matter for him to *remain* rich. Dab-Dab used to say that during the years she had known him he had, to her knowledge, been quite well off five or six times; but that the more money he had, the sooner you could expect him to be poor again.

Well, the point from which we are beginning, then, is where the Dolittle party (Jip the dog, Dab-Dab the duck, Too-Too the owl, Gub-Gub the pig, the pushmi-pullyu and the white mouse) had returned at last to the little house in Puddleby-on-the-Marsh after their long journey from Africa. It was a large family to find food for. And the Doctor, without a penny in his pockets, had been a good deal worried over how he was going to feed it, even during the short time they would be here before arrangements were made to join a circus. However, the thoughtful Dab-Dab had made them carry up from the ship such supplies as remained in the larder after the voyage was done. These, she said, should last the household – with economy – for a day or two at least.

Although the people in Puddleby had not yet learned of the

Doctor's arrival, news of his coming had already spread among the animals and the birds. All that afternoon he was kept busy bandaging, advising and physicking, while a huge motley crowd of creatures waited patiently outside the surgery door.

'Ah me! – just like old times,' sighed Dab-Dab. 'No peace. Patients clamouring to see him morning, noon and night.'

By the time darkness came that night it was very chilly. Wood enough was found in the cellar to start a jolly fire in the big chimney. Round this the animals gathered after supper and pestered the Doctor for a story or a chapter from one of his books.

'But look here,' said he. 'What about the circus? If we're going to make money to pay the sailor back we've got to be thinking of that. We haven't even found a circus to go with yet. I wonder what's the best way to set about it. They travel all over the place, you know. Let me see: who could I ask?'

'Sh!' said Too-Too. 'Wasn't that the front doorbell ringing?'

'Strange!' said the Doctor, getting up from his chair. 'Callers already?'

'Perhaps it's the old lady with rheumatism,' said the white mouse as the Doctor walked out into the hall. 'Maybe she didn't find her Oxenthorpe doctor was so very good after all.'

When John Dolittle had lit the candles in the hall he opened the front door. And there standing on the threshold was the Cat's-meat-Man.

'Why, it's Matthew Mugg, as I'm alive!' he cried. 'Come in, Matthew, come in. But how did you know I was here?'

'I felt it in my bones, Doctor,' said the Cat's-meat-Man, stumping into the hall. 'Only this morning I says to my wife, "Theodosia," I says, "something tells me the Doctor's got back. And I'm going up to his house tonight to take a look." '

'Well, I'm glad to see you,' said John Dolittle. 'Let's go into the kitchen where it's warm.'

Although he said he had only come on the chance of finding the Doctor, the Cat's-meat-Man had brought presents with him: a knuckle-bone off a shoulder of mutton for Jip; a piece of cheese for the white mouse; a turnip for Gub-Gub and a pot of

'Why, it's Matthew Mugg!'

flowering geraniums for the Doctor. When the visitor was comfortably settled in the armchair before the fire John Dolittle handed him the tobacco-jar from the mantelpiece and told him to fill his pipe.

'Are you home for a long stay now?' asked Matthew.

'Well – yes and no,' said the Doctor. 'I'd like nothing better than to enjoy a few quiet months here and get my garden to rights. It's in a shocking mess. But unfortunately I've got to make some money first.'

'Humph,' said Matthew, puffing at his pipe. 'Meself, I've bin trying to do that all my life. Never was very good at it. But I've got twenty-five shillings saved up, if that would help you.'

'It's very kind of you, Matthew, very. The fact is I – er – I need a whole lot of money. I've got to pay back some debts. But listen: I have a strange kind of new animal – a pushmi-pullyu. He has two heads. The monkeys in Africa presented him to me after I had cured an epidemic for them. Their idea was that I should travel with him in a circus – on show, you know. Would you like to see him?'

'I surely would,' said the Cat's meat-Man. 'Sounds like something very new.'

'He's out in the garden,' said the Doctor. 'Don't stare at him too hard. He isn't used to it yet. Gets frightfully embarrassed. Let's take a bucket of water with us and just pretend we've brought him a drink.'

When Matthew came back into the kitchen with the Doctor he was all smiles and enthusiasm.

'Why, John Dolittle,' said he, 'you'll make your fortune – sure as you're alive! There's never bin anything seen like that since the world began. And anyway, I always thought you ought to go into the circus business – you, the only man living that knows animal-language. When are you going to start?'

'That's just the point. Perhaps you can help me. I'd want to be sure it was a nice circus I was going with – people I would like, you understand.'

Matthew Mugg bent forward and tapped the Doctor on the knee with the stem of his pipe.

'I know the very concern you want,' said he. 'Right now over at Grimbledon there's the nicest little circus you ever saw. Grimbledon Fair's on this week and they'll be there till Saturday. Me and Theodosia saw 'em the first day they was on. It isn't a large circus but it's a good one – select like. What do you say if I take you over there tomorrow and you have a chat with the ringmaster?'

'Why that would be splendid,' said the Doctor. 'But in the meantime don't say anything to anyone about the idea at all.

We must keep the pushmi-pullyu a secret till he is actually put on show before the public.'

BUSINESS ARRANGEMENTS

THE next day Matthew Mugg and the Doctor set out for Grimbledon. They found the manager of the circus, Alexander Blossom, counting money at the gate.

John Dolittle described the wonderful animal that he had at home and said he wanted to join the circus with him. Alexander Blossom admitted he would like to see the creature, and told the Doctor to bring him here. But John Dolittle said it would be better and easier if the manager came to Puddleby to look at him.

This was agreed upon. And after they had explained to Blossom how to get to the little house on the Oxenthorpe Road, they set out for home again, very pleased with their success so far.

'If you do go with Blossom's Circus,' Matthew asked, as they tramped along the road chewing sardine sandwiches, 'will you take me with you, Doctor? I'd come in real handy, taking care of the caravan, feeding and cleaning and the likes o' that.'

'You're very welcome to come, Matthew,' said the Doctor. 'But what about your own business?'

'Oh, that,' said Matthew, biting viciously into another sandwich. 'There ain't no money in that. Besides, it's so tame, handing out bits of meat on skewers to overfed poodles! There's no – no what d'y' call it?' – (he waved his sandwich towards the sky) – 'no adventure in it. I'm naturally venturesome – reckless like – always was, from my cradle up. Now the circus: that's real life! That's a man's job.'

'But how about your wife?' asked the Doctor.

'Theodosia? Oh, she'd come along. She's venturesome, like me. She could mend the clothes and do odd jobs. What do you think?'

'I think that would be fine, Matthew,' said the Doctor.

He waved his sandwich towards the sky

Late that night, when the Grimbledon Fair had closed, Mr Blossom, the ringmaster, came to the Doctor's house in Puddleby.

After he had been shown by the light of a lantern the pushmi-pullyu grazing on the lawn, he came back into the library with the Doctor and said:

'How much do you want for that animal?'

'No, no, he's not for sale,' said the Doctor.

'Oh, come now,' said the manager. 'You don't want him. Anyone could see you're not a regular showman. I'll give you twenty pounds for him.'

'No,' said the Doctor.

'Thirty pounds,' said Blossom.

Still the Doctor refused.

'Forty pounds – fifty pounds,' said the manager. Then he went up and up, offering prices that made the Cat's-meat-Man who was listening open his eyes wider and wider with wonder.

'It's no use,' said the Doctor at last. 'You must either take me with the animal into your circus or leave him where he is. I have promised that I myself will see he is properly treated.'

'What do you mean?' asked the showman. 'Ain't he your property? Who did you promise?'

'He's his own property,' said the Doctor. 'He came here to oblige me. It was to himself, the pushmi-pullyu, that I gave my promise.'

'What! – Are you crazy?' asked the showman.

Matthew Mugg was going to explain to Blossom that the Doctor could speak animals' language. But John Dolittle motioned to him to be silent.

'And so, you see,' he went on, 'you must either take me *and* the animal or neither.'

Well, the upshot of it was that the showman finally consented to all the Doctor asked. The pushmi-pullyu and his party were to be provided with a new wagon all to themselves and, although travelling as part of the circus, were to be entirely free and independent. The money made was to be divided equally between the Doctor and the manager. Whenever the pushmi-pullyu wanted a day off he was to have it, and whatever kind of food he asked for was to be provided by Blossom.

When all the arrangements had been gone into, the man said he would send the caravan here next day, and prepared to go. 'Have your party ready by eleven in the morning. Good night.'

'Good night,' said the Doctor.

CIRCUS LIFE

VERY early the next morning Dab-Dab had the whole house astir. The diligent housekeeper had the house closed and everybody waiting outside on the front steps hours before the wagon arrived. But the Doctor, for one, was still kept busy. For up to the last minute animal patients were still coming in from all parts of the countryside, with various ailments to be cured.

At last Jip, who had been out scouting, came rushing back to the party gathered on the steps.

'The wagon's coming,' he panted, 'all red and yellow – it's just around the bend.'

Then everybody got excited and began grabbing the parcels. Gub-Gub's luggage was a bundle of turnips; and just as he was hurrying down the steps to the road the string broke and the round, white vegetables went rolling all over the place.

The wagon, when it finally came in sight, was certainly a thing of beauty. It was made like a gypsy caravan, with windows and door and chimney. It was very gaily painted and quite new.

Not so the horse; he was quite old. The Doctor said that never had he seen an animal so worn out and weary. He got into conversation with him and found out that he had been working in the circus for thirty-five years. He was very sick of it he said. His name was Beppo. The Doctor decided he would tell Blossom that it was high time Beppo should be pensioned off and allowed to live in peace.

When the animals and the baggage were all in, the Doctor got terribly afraid that the load would be too much for the old horse to pull. And he wanted to push behind, to help. But Beppo said he could manage it all right. However, the Doctor would not add to the weight by getting in himself. And when the door was shut and the window curtains drawn, so no one should see the pushmi-pullyu on the way, they set out for Grimbledon,

Waiting on the front steps

with the man who had brought the wagon driving and the Doctor and the Cat's-meat-Man walking behind.

They reached the Grimbledon Fair-grounds about two o'clock in the afternoon and entered the circus enclosure by a back gate. Inside they found the great Blossom himself, waiting to welcome them.

He seemed quite surprised, on the van's being opened, to find the odd collection of creatures the Doctor had brought with him – he was particularly astonished at the pig. However, he was so delighted to have the pushmi-pullyu that he didn't mind.

He at once led them to what he called their stand – which, he said, he had had built for them that very morning. This the Doctor found to be similar to the place where he had first spoken with Blossom. It was a platform raised three feet from the ground, so that the board-and-canvas room on the top of it could be seen. It had steps up to it, and a little way back from the front edge of the platform curtains covered the entrance to the room, so no one could see inside unless they paid to go in.

Across the front of it was a sign:

THE PUSHMI-PULLYU!
COME AND SEE THE MARVELLOUS
TWO-HEADED ANIMAL
FROM THE JUNGLES OF AFRICA!
ADMISSION SIXPENCE

The red and yellow wagon (in which the Doctor's party, with the exception of the pushmi-pullyu, were to live) was backed behind the 'stand'. And Dab-Dab immediately set about making up beds and arranging the inside so it would be homelike.

After the pushmi-pullyu had been moved to his new home in the stand and the Doctor had seen that he was provided with hay and water and bedding, the Puddleby party started out to make a tour of the circus under the guidance of the great Alexander Blossom, ringmaster.

The main show took place only twice a day in a big tent in the middle of the enclosure. But all around this there were smaller tents and stands, most of which you had to pay extra to get into. Of these the Doctor's establishment was now to form one. They contained all manner of wonders: shooting galleries; guessing games; wild men of Borneo; bearded ladies; merry-go-rounds; strong men; snake charmers; a menagerie and many more.

Blossom took the Doctor and his friends to the menagerie first. It was a dingy third-rate sort of collection. Most of the animals seemed dirty and unhappy. The Doctor was so saddened he was all for having a row with Blossom over it. But the Cat's-meat-Man whispered in his ear:

The wagon was backed behind the stand

'Don't be starting trouble right away, Doctor. Wait a while. After the boss sees how valuable you are with performing animals you'll be able to do what you like with him. If you kick up a shindy now we'll maybe lose our job. Then you won't be able to do anything.'

This struck John Dolittle as good advice. And he contented himself for the present with whispering to the animals through the bars of their cages that later he hoped to do something for them.

Just as they had entered, a dirty man was taking around a group of country folk to show them the collection. Stopping before a cage where a small furry animal was imprisoned, the man called out:

'And this, ladies and gents, is the famous Hurri-Gurri, from the forests of Patagonia. 'E 'angs from the trees by 'is tail. Pass on to the next cage.'

The Doctor, followed by Gub-Gub, went over and looked in at 'the famous Hurri-Gurri'.

'Why,' said he, 'that's nothing but a common opossum from America. One of the marsupials.'

'How do you know it's a Ma Soupial, Doctor?' asked Gub-Gub. 'She hasn't any children with her. Perhaps it's a Pa Soupial.'

'And this,' roared the man, standing before the next cage, 'is the largest elephant in captivity.'

'Almost the smallest one I ever saw,' murmured the Doctor.

Then Mr Blossom suggested that they go on to the next show, Princess Fatima, the snake charmer. And he led the way out of the close, evil-smelling menagerie into the open air. As the Doctor passed down the line of cages he hung his head, frowning unhappily. For the various animals, recognizing the great John Dolittle, were all making signs to him to stop and talk with them.

When they entered the snake charmer's tent there were no other visitors there for the moment but themselves. On the small stage they beheld the Princess Fatima, powdering her large nose and swearing to herself in cockney. Beside her chair was a big shallow box full of snakes. Matthew Mugg peeped into it, gasped in horror, and then started to run from the tent.

'It's all right, Matthew,' the Doctor called out. 'Don't be alarmed, they're quite harmless.'

'What d'yer mean, harmless?' snorted the Princess Fatima, glaring at the Doctor. 'They're king cobras, from India – the deadliest snakes livin'.'

'They're nothing of the sort,' said the Doctor. 'They're American blacksnakes – non-poisonous.' And he tickled one under the chin.

'Leave them snakes alone!' yelled Fatima, rising from her chair, 'or I'll knock yer bloomin' 'ead orf.'

Crossing over to the strong man's booth, Gub-Gub caught sight of the Punch and Judy show which was going on at that moment. The play had just reached that point where Toby the dog bites Mr Punch on the nose. Gub-Gub was fascinated. They could hardly drag him away from it. Indeed, throughout the whole time they spent with the circus this was his chief delight. He never missed a single performance – and although the play was always the same and he got to know it every word by heart, he never grew tired of it.

At the next booth a large audience was gathered and yokels were gasping in wonder as the strong man lifted enormous weights in the air. There was no fake about this show. And John Dolittle, deeply interested, joined in the clapping and the gasping.

The strong man was an honest-looking fellow, with tremendous muscles. The Doctor took a liking to him right away. One of his tricks was to lie on the stage on his back and lift an enormous dumb-bell with his feet till his legs were sticking right up in the air. It needed balance as well as strength, because if the dumb-bell should fall the wrong way the man would certainly be injured. Today when he had finally brought his legs into an upright position and the crowd was whispering in admiration, suddenly there was a loud crack. One of the boards of the stage had given way. Instantly down came the big dumb-bell right across the man's chest.

The crowd screamed and Blossom jumped up on the platform. It took two men's strength to lift the dumb-bell off the strong man's body. But even then he did not arise. He lay motionless, his eyes closed, his face a deathly white.

'Get a doctor,' Blossom shouted to the Cat's-meat-Man. 'Hurry! He's hurt hisself – unconscious. A doctor, quick!'

But John Dolittle was already on the stage, standing over the ringmaster, who knelt beside the injured man.

'Get out of the way and let me examine him,' he said quietly.

'What can you do? He's hurt bad. Look, his breathing's queer. We got to get a doctor.'

'I am a doctor,' said John Dolittle. 'Matthew, run to the van and get my black bag.'

'You a doctor!' said Blossom, getting up off his knees.

'Of course, he's a doctor,' came a voice out of the crowd. 'There wur a time when he wur the best-known doctor in the West Country. I know un. Dolittle's his name – John Dolittle, of Puddleby-on-the-Marsh.'

The Doctor found that two of the strong man's ribs had been broken by the dumb-bell. However, he prophesied that with so powerful a constitution the patient should recover quickly. The injured man was put to bed in his own caravan and until he was well again the Doctor visited him four times a day and Matthew slept in his wagon to nurse him.

The strong man (his show name was Hercules) was very thankful to John Dolittle and became greatly attached to him.

The next day, the pushmi-pullyu was put on show for the first time. He was very popular. A two-headed animal had never before been seen in a circus and the people thronged up to pay their money and have a look at him. At first he nearly died of embarrassment and shyness, and he was for ever hiding one of his heads under the straw so as not to have to meet the gaze of all those staring eyes. Then the people wouldn't believe he had more than one head. So the Doctor asked him if he would be so good as to keep both of them in view.

'You need not look at the people,' he said. 'But just let them see that you really have two heads. You can turn your back on the audience – both ends.'

But some of the silly people, even when they could see the two heads plainly, kept saying that one must be faked. And they would prod the poor, timid animal with sticks to see if part of him was stuffed. While two country bumpkins were doing this one day the pushmi-pullyu got annoyed, and bringing both his heads up sharply at the same time, he jabbed the two inquirers in the legs. Then they knew for sure that he was real and alive all over.

But as soon as the Cat's-meat-Man could be spared from nursing Hercules (he turned the job over to his wife) the Doctor put him on guard inside the stall to see that the animal was not molested by stupid visitors. The poor creature had a terrible time those first days. But when Jip told him how much money was being taken in, he determined to stick it out for John Dolittle's sake. And after a little while, although his opinion of the human race sank very low, he got sort of used to the silly, gaping faces of his audiences and gazed back at them – from both his heads – with fearless superiority and the scorn that they deserved.

DOCTOR DOLITTLE MEETS SOPHIE

ONE night on a trip between towns the procession had stopped by the side of the road as usual. There was a nice old-fashioned farm quite near and Gub-Gub had gone off to see if there were any pigs in the sty. Otherwise the Doctor's family circle was complete. And soon after the kettle had been put on to boil, Jip's two friends, Toby the Punch-and-Judy dog and Swizzle the clown's dog, came to the caravan and joined the Doctor's family.

The night was cool; so, instead of making a fire outside, Dab-Dab was using the stove in the caravan, and everybody was sitting around it chatting.

'Have you heard the news, Doctor?' said Toby, jumping up on the bed.

'No,' said John Dolittle. 'What is it?'

'At the next town – Ashby, you know, quite a large place – we are to pick up Sophie.'

'Who in the world is Sophie?' asked the Doctor, getting out his slippers from behind the stove.

'She left us before you joined,' said Swizzle. 'Sophie's the performing seal – balances balls on her nose and does tricks in the water. She fell sick and Blossom had to leave her behind about a month ago. She's all right now, though, and her keeper is meeting us at Ashby so she can join us again. She's rather a sentimental sort of girl, is Sophie. But she's a good sport, and I'm sure you will like her.'

The circus reached the town of Ashby at nine o'clock the next morning. After the tents were all rigged and everything in readiness for the afternoon performance, Doctor Dolittle set out to make the acquaintance of the performing seal.

Sophie, a fine five-foot Alaskan seal, with sleek skin and intelligent eyes, was one of the features of the big tent twice a day. During the rest of the time she was kept in a tank which was let into the ground. Visitors could watch her dive for fish for their amusement if they paid threepence to come and see her.

When the Doctor arrived at the railing which surrounded the tank he spoke to her in her own language.

She burst into a flood of tears when she realized who the Doctor was.

'What is the matter?' asked John Dolittle.

The seal, still weeping, did not answer.

'Calm yourself,' said the Doctor. 'Don't be hysterical. Tell me, are you still sick? I understood you had recovered.'

'Oh, yes, I got over that,' said Sophie through her tears. 'It was only an upset stomach. They *will* feed us this stale fish, you know.'

'Then what's the matter?' asked the Doctor. 'Why are you crying?'

'I was weeping for joy,' said Sophie. 'I was just thinking as you came in that the only person in the world who could help me in my trouble was John Dolittle. Of course, I had heard all about you through the Post Office and the *Arctic Monthly*. In fact, I had written to you. It was I who contributed those articles on under-water swimming – you remember? – The Alaskan Wiggle, you know – double overhand stroke. It was printed in the August number of your magazine. We were awfully sorry when you had to give up the *Arctic Monthly*. It was tremendously popular among the seals.'

'But what was this trouble you were speaking of?' asked the Doctor.

'Oh yes,' said Sophie, bursting into tears again. 'That just shows you how glad I am; I had forgotten all about it for the moment. You know, when you first came in I thought you were an ordinary visitor. But the very first word of sealish that you spoke – and Alaskan sealish at that – I knew who you were: John Dolittle, the one man in the world I wanted to see. It was too much, I –'

'Come, come!' said the Doctor. 'Don't break down again. Tell me what your trouble is.'

'When I was sick they decided I needed company. So they put me in a pond with the other seals until I should recover.'

Sophie began to weep again. But she pulled herself together and went on: 'One of the seals who had come from the Behring Straits as I did told me that my husband has refused to eat since I was captured and brought here. He used to be leader of the herd and now another seal was elected in his place. Poor Slushy! My poor, poor Slushy!'

'Poor who?' asked the Doctor.

'Slushy,' said the seal. 'That's my husband's name. He relied on me for everything – poor, simple Slushy. What shall I do? What *shall* I do? I ought to go to him.'

'Well, now listen,' said John Dolittle. 'It's not an easy matter to arrange a trip to Alaska. Perhaps I can persuade Mr Higgins, your keeper, to let you visit – er, Slushy.'

The Doctor thought a minute. He leaned over the railing and spoke in seal-language.

'Cheer up!' he said. 'I'll find a way.'

Just then a schoolmistress with a band of children entered,

'I ought to go to him'

accompanied by Higgins, the keeper. As he came in the Doctor went out, smiling to himself. Soon the children were laughing with delight at the antics in the tank. And Higgins decided that Sophie must be feeling entirely recovered, for he had never seen her so sprightly or so full of good spirits.

The Doctor returned to the caravan and asked Toby the Punch-and-Judy dog:

'Does Sophie belong to Blossom or to Higgins?'

'To Higgins, Doctor,' said the little dog. 'He does something the same as you do; in return for letting the seal perform in the big ring, Higgins gets his stand in the circus free, and pockets whatever money he makes on her as a side show.'

'Well, that *isn't* the same as me at all,' said the Doctor. 'The big difference is that the pushmi-pullyu is here of his own accord and Sophie is kept against her will. It is a perfect scandal that hunters can go up to the Arctic and capture any animals they like, breaking up families and upsetting herd government and community life in this way – a crying shame! Toby, how much does a seal cost?'

'They vary in price, Doctor,' said Toby. 'But I heard Sophie say that when Higgins bought her in Liverpool from the men who had caught her he paid twenty pounds for her. She had been trained on the ship to do tricks before she landed.'

'How much have we got in the money-box, Too-Too?' asked the Doctor.

'All of last week's gate money,' said the owl, 'except one shilling and threepence. The threepence you spent to get your hair cut and the shilling went on celery for Gub-Gub.'

'Well, what does that bring the total to?'

Too-Too, the mathematician, cocked his head on one side and closed his left eye – as he always did when calculating.

'Two pounds, seven shillings,' he murmured, 'minus one shilling and threepence leaves – er – leaves – two pounds five shillings and ninepence, cash in hand, net.'

'Good Lord!' groaned the Doctor, 'barely enough to buy a tenth of Sophie! I wonder if there's anyone I could borrow from. That's the only good thing about being a doctor. When I had a practice I could borrow from my patients.'

'If I remember rightly,' muttered Dab-Dab, 'it was more often your patients that borrowed from you.'

'Blossom wouldn't let you buy her even if you had the money,' said Swizzle. 'Higgins is under contract – made a promise – to travel with the circus for a year.'

'Very well, then,' said the Doctor. 'There's only one thing to be done. That seal doesn't belong to those men, anyhow. She's a free citizen of the Arctic Circle. And if she wants to go back there, back she shall go. Sophie must escape.'

PLANNING THE ESCAPE

ALTHOUGH the plans for Sophie's escape were of course kept a strict secret from any of the people in Blossom's establishment, the animals of the circus soon got to know of them through Jip, Toby and Swizzle.

The plan was for the Doctor to leave the circus a few days ahead of Sophie so that Blossom would not connect her escape with the Doctor. In this way no one would be searching for John Dolittle but would simply be giving chase to an escaped seal.

When the Doctor returned from announcing to the manager that he was about to leave the circus on business he found the animals seated about the table in the caravan and talking in whispers.

'Well, Doctor,' said Matthew, who was sitting on the steps, 'did you speak to the boss?'

'Yes,' said the Doctor. 'I told him. It's all right. I'm leaving tonight. I felt frightfully guilty, and underhanded. I do wish I could do this openly.'

'You'd stand a fat chance of succeeding, if you did!' said Matthew. 'I don't feel guilty at all.'

'Listen, Doctor,' said Jip. 'Let me know if there's anything I can do to help. When is Sophie going to get away?'

'The day after tomorrow,' said John Dolittle. 'Matthew, here, will undo the door of her stand just after closing time. But listen, Matthew: you'll have to be awfully careful no one sees you tinkering with the lock. If we *should* get caught we would indeed be in a bad fix then. Tinkering with locks makes it a felony instead of a misdemeanour, or something like that. Do be careful, won't you?'

'You can rely on me, Doctor,' said the Cat's-meat-Man, proudly puffing out his chest. 'I've got a way of me own with locks, I have. No force, sort of persuasion like.'

'Get clear out of the way as soon as you have let her free,' said

Swizzle bowed to an imaginary audience

the Doctor, 'so you won't be connected with it at all. Dear me, how like a low-down conspiracy it sounds!'

'Sounds like lots of fun to me,' said Matthew.

'To me too,' said Jip.

'It'll be the best trick that's been done in this show for a long while,' put in Swizzle. 'Ladies and Gentlemen: John Dolittle, the world-famous conjurer, will now make a live seal disappear from the stage before your eyes. Abracadabra, Mumble-and-Jabberer, Hoop la – Hey Presto! – *Gone.*'

And Swizzle stood on his hind legs and bowed to an imaginary audience behind the stove.

'Well,' said the Doctor, 'even though it sounds underhanded, I don't feel I'm doing anything wrong – myself. They've no right to keep Sophie in this slavery. How would you like it,' he asked of Matthew, 'to be made to dive for fish into a tub of dirty water for the amusement of loafers?'

'Rotten!' said Matthew. 'I never did care for fish – nor water, neither. But look here, have you arranged with Sophie where she's to meet you?'

'Yes,' said John Dolittle. 'As soon as she gets clear of the circus enclosure – and don't forget we are relying on you to leave the back gate open as well as Sophie's own door – as soon as she's out of the fence, she is to cross the road where she will find an empty house. Alongside of that there is a little, dark passage, and in that passage I will be waiting for her. My goodness, I do hope everything goes right! It's so dreadfully important for her and her husband in Alaska, too.'

'And what are you going to do then,' asked Matthew, 'when she's got as far as the passage?'

'Well, it's no use trying to plan too far as to detail. My general idea is to make for the Bristol Channel. That's about our shortest cut to the sea from here. Once there, she's all right. But it's nearly a hundred miles as the crow flies; and as we'll have to keep concealed most of the way I'm not expecting an easy journey. However, there's no sense in meeting your troubles halfway. I've no doubt we shall get along all right once she's safely away from the circus.'

So that night after a final talk with Sophie he set out alone – on business. He took with him most of what money he had, leaving a little with Matthew to pay for the small needs of his establishment while he was away. His 'business' as a matter of fact did not take him farther than the next town – which journey he made by a stagecoach.

On his arrival at the next town he took a room in an inn and remained there the whole time. Two nights later he returned to Ashby after dark and, entering the town from the far side, made his way through unfrequented streets till he reached the passage which was to be his meeting place with Sophie.

IN THE DESERTED GARDEN

In spite of everything that Theodosia, Matthew's wife, could do to distract the night watchman while the Cat's-meat-Man unlocked Sophie's stand, she was unable to detain him very long. He took his lamp and left on his rounds. Higgins, who had been chatting with them, however, remained.

It was but a few minutes before the watchman came running back to Matthew's wagon.

'Higgins,' he yelled, 'your seal's gone!'

'Gone!' cried Higgins.

'Gone!' said Theodosia. 'Can't be possible!'

'I tell you she has,' said the watchman. ' 'Er door's open and she ain't there.'

'Good heavens!' cried Higgins springing up. 'I could swear I locked the door as usual. But if the gate in the fence was still closed she can't be far away. Come on!'

And he ran out of the wagon. By this time Matthew had joined them and he and Theodosia, pretending to be greatly disturbed, followed close behind.

They all raced for the seal's stand.

'The door's open, sure enough,' said Matthew as they came up to it. ' 'Ow very peculiar!'

'Let's go inside,' said Higgins. 'Maybe she's hiding at the bottom of the tank.'

The watchman raised his lamp and they all peered into the dark water.

'There ain't nothing under the water,' said Higgins. 'Sophie's not here.'

Meanwhile, John Dolittle, waiting anxious and impatient, in the dark passage, heard to his delight the sound of a peculiar footstep. A flipper-step, it should more properly be called; for the noise of Sophie travelling over pavement was a curious mixture between someone slapping the ground with a wet rag and a sack of potatoes being yanked along a floor.

'Is that you, Sophie?' he whispered.

'Yes,' said the seal, hitching herself forward to where the Doctor stood.

'Thank goodness!' he said, 'I was afraid you might not get away.'

'Oh, I got away all right,' said Sophie. 'But hadn't we better get out of town? It doesn't seem to me very safe here.'

'There's no chance of that for the present,' said the Doctor. 'The noise they made in the circus has woken everybody. We dare not try and get through the streets now. I just saw a policeman pass across the end of the passage there – luckily for us, just after you popped into it.'

'But then what are we going to do?'

'We'll have to stay here for the present. It would be madness to try and run for it now.'

'Well, but suppose they come searching in here. We couldn't –'

At that moment two persons with lanterns stopped at the end of the passage, talked a moment and moved away.

'Quite so,' whispered the Doctor. 'This isn't safe either. We must find a better place.'

Now, on one side of this alleyway there was a high stone wall and on the other a high brick wall. The brick wall enclosed the back garden belonging to the deserted house.

'If we could only get into that old empty house,' murmured the Doctor. 'We'd be safe to stay there as long as we wished – till this excitement at the circus dies down. Can you think of any way you could get over that wall?'

The seal measured the height with her eye.

'Eight feet,' she murmured. 'I could do it with a ladder. I've been trained to walk up ladders. I do it in the circus, you know. Perhaps –'

'Sh!' whispered the Doctor. 'Listen, there's just a chance I may find an orchard ladder in the garden. Now you wait here, lie flat and wait till I come back.'

His fingers caught the top of it

Then John Dolittle, a very active man in spite of his round figure, drew back and took a running jump at the wall. His fingers caught the top of it; he hauled himself up, threw one leg over and dropped lightly down into a flower-bed on the other side. At the bottom of the garden he saw in the moonlight what he guessed to be a tool-shed. Slipping up to the door, he opened it and went in. He lit a match.

And there, sure enough, hanging against the wall right above his head, was an orchard ladder, just the right length. In a moment he had blown out the match, opened the door and was marching down the garden with the ladder on his shoulder.

Standing it in a firm place, he scaled up and sat astride the wall. Next he pulled the ladder up after him, changed it across to the other side and lowered the foot-end into the passage.

Then John Dolittle, perched astride the top of the wall (looking exactly like Humpty Dumpty) whispered down into the dark passage below him:

'Now climb up. Sophie, I'll keep this end steady. And when you reach the top get on to the wall beside me till I change the ladder over to the garden side. Don't get flustered now. Easy does it.'

It was a good thing that Sophie was so well trained in balancing. Never in the circus had she performed a better trick than she did that night. It was a feat that even a person might well be proud of. But she knew that her freedom, the happiness of her husband, depended on her steadiness. And, though she was in constant fear that any minute someone might come down the passage and discover them, it gave her a real thrill to turn the tables on her captors by using the skill they had taught her in this last grand performance to escape them.

Firmly, rung by rung, she began hoisting her heavy body upward. The ladder, fortunately, was longer than the height of the wall. Thus the Doctor had been able to set it at an easier, flattish slope, instead of straight upright. With the seal's weight it sagged dangerously; and the Doctor on the wall prayed that it would prove strong enough. Being an orchard ladder, for tree-pruning, it got very narrow at the top. And it was here, where there was hardly room enough for a seal's two front flappers to take hold, that the ticklish part of the feat came in. Then, from this awkward situation Sophie had to shift her clumsy bulk on to the wall, which was no more than twelve inches wide, while the Doctor changed the ladder.

But in the circus Sophie had been trained to balance herself on small spaces, as well as to climb ladders. And after the Doctor had helped her by leaning down and hoisting her up by the slack of her sealskin jacket, she wiggled herself along the

He lowered the ladder into the garden

top of the wall beside him and kept her balance as easily as though it were nothing at all.

Then, while Sophie gave a fine imitation of a statue in the moonlight, the Doctor hauled the ladder up after her, swung it over – knocking his own high hat off in the process – and lowered it into the garden once more.

Coming down, Sophie did another of her show tricks; she laid herself across the ladder and slid to the bottom. It was quicker than climbing.

'Do you think we'll be able to get away soon, Doctor?' asked Sophie. 'I'm anxious to get started.'

'I hope so,' said the Doctor. 'But we must wait until things quiet down. Try and be patient.'

About half an hour later the Doctor took the ladder and, mounting near the top of the garden wall, he listened long and carefully.

'There are still an awful lot of people moving about in the streets,' he said. 'But whether they are circus men hunting you, or just ordinary townsfolk walking abroad, I can't make out. We'd better wait a while longer, I think.'

'Oh, dear!' sighed Sophie. 'Are we never going to get farther than this garden? Poor Slushy! I'm so worried.' And she began to weep softly.

After another hour had gone by, the Doctor went out again. This time, just as he was about to climb the ladder, he heard Jip whispering to him on the other side of the wall.

'Doctor, are you there?'

'Yes, what is it?'

'Listen! Higgins and the boss have gone off somewhere with a wagon. Blossom just came and told Matthew to take on some extra jobs with the circus because he wouldn't be back for a while. Too-Too thinks it's a grand chance for you to make a dash for it and get out of the town. Have you got that?'

'Yes, I heard you, thank you, Jip. All right. We'll leave in fifteen minutes.' And the Doctor looked at his watch. 'Which way did Blossom go?'

'East – towards Grimbledon. Swizzle followed them out a ways and came back and told us. You make for the west. Can you hear me?'

'Yes, I understand,' whispered the Doctor. Then he told Sophie to be ready.

'Now, listen,' said the Doctor, 'if we meet anyone on the street – and we are pretty sure to – you lie down by the wall and pretend you're a sack I'm carrying – that I'm taking a rest, you see. Try and look as much like a sack as you can. Understand?'

'All right,' said Sophie. 'I'm frightfully excited. See how my flippers are fluttering.'

Well, the Doctor kept an eye on his watch; and long before the minutes had passed he and Sophie were waiting at the foot of the ladder ready and impatient.

Finally, after looking at the time once more, the Doctor whispered:

'All right, I think we can start now. Let me go first, so I can steady the ladder for you, the way I did before.'

But, alas, for poor Sophie's hopes! Just as the Doctor was half-way up, the noise of distant barking, deep-voiced and angry, broke out.

John Dolittle paused on the ladder, frowning. The barking, many dogs baying together, drew nearer.

'What's that?' said Sophie in a tremulous whisper from below. 'That's not Jip or any of our dogs.'

'No,' said the Doctor, climbing down slowly. 'There's no mistaking that sound. Sophie, something's gone wrong. That's the baying of bloodhounds – bloodhounds on a scent. And they're coming – this way!'

THE LEADER OF THE BLOODHOUNDS

JIP, after his last conversation with the Doctor over the garden wall, returned to the caravan with his friends, feeling comfortably sure that now everything would go all right.

He and Too-Too were chatting under the table while Dab-Dab was dusting the furniture, when suddenly in rushed Toby, all out of breath.

'Jip,' he cried. 'The worst has happened! They've got bloodhounds. That's what Blossom and Higgins went off for. There's a man who raises them, it seems in the next village. They're bringing 'em here in a wagon – six of 'em. I spotted them just as they entered the town over the toll-bridge. I ran behind and tried to speak to the dogs. But with the rattle of the wagon-wheels they couldn't hear me. If they put those hounds on Sophie's trail she's as good as caught already.'

'Confound them!' muttered Jip. 'Where are they now, Toby?'

'I don't know. When I left them they were crossing the market-place on their way here at the trot. I raced ahead to let you know as quick as I could.'

'All right,' said Jip, springing up. 'Come with me.'

And he dashed out into the night.

'They'll try and pick up the trail from the seal's stand,' said Jip as the two dogs ran on together across the enclosure. 'Perhaps we can meet them there.'

But at the stand there were no bloodhounds.

Jip put his nose to the ground and sniffed just once.

'Drat the luck!' he whispered. 'They've been here already and gone off on the trail. Listen, there they are, baying now. Come on! Let's race for the passage. We may be in time yet.'

And away he sped like a white arrow towards the gate, while poor little Toby, left far behind, with his flappy ears trailing in the wind, put on his best speed to keep up.

Dashing into the passage, Jip found it simply full of men and dogs and lanterns. Blossom was there, and Higgins and the man who owned the hounds. While the men talked and waved the lamps, the hounds, six great, droopy-jowled beasts, with long ears and bloodshot eyes, sniffed the ground and ran hither and thither about the alley, trying to find where the trail led out. Every once in a while they would lift their noses, open their big mouths and send a deep-voiced howl rolling towards the moon.

By this time other dogs in the neighbourhood were answering their bark from every backyard. Jip ran into the crowded passage, pretending to join in the hunt for scent. Picking out the biggest bloodhound, who, he guessed, was the leader, he got alongside him. Then, still keeping his eyes and nose to the ground, he whispered in dog language:

'Get your duffers out of here. This is the Doctor's business – John Dolittle's.'

The bloodhound paused and eyed Jip haughtily.

'Who are you, mongrel?'

'Who are you, mongrel?' he said. 'We've been set to run down a seal. Stop trying to fool us. John Dolittle is away on a voyage.'

'He's nothing of the kind,' muttered Jip. 'He's on the other side of the wall – not six feet away from us. He is trying to get this seal down to the sea, so she can escape these men with the lanterns – if you idiots will only get out of the way.'

'I don't believe you,' said the leader. 'The last I heard of the Doctor he was travelling in Africa. We must do our duty.'

'Duffer! Numskull!' growled Jip, losing his temper entirely. 'I'm telling you the truth. For two pins I'd pull your long ears.

You must have been asleep in your kennel the last two years. The Doctor's been back in England over a month. He's travelling with the circus now.'

But the leader of the bloodhounds, like many trained specialists, was (in everything outside his own profession) very obstinate and a bit stupid. He just simply would not believe that the Doctor wasn't still abroad. In all his famous record as a tracker he had never failed to run down his quarry, once he took up a scent. He had a big reputation, and was proud of it. He wasn't going to be misled by every whipper-snapper of a dog who came along with an idle tale – no, not he.

Poor Jip was in despair. He saw that the hounds were now sniffing at the wall over which Sophie had climbed. He knew that these great beasts would never leave this neighbourhood while the seal was near and her fishy scent so strong all about. It was only a matter of time before Blossom and Higgins would guess that she was hiding beyond the wall and would have the old house and garden searched.

While he was still arguing, an idea came to Jip. He left the knot of bloodhounds and nosed his way carelessly down to the bottom of the passage. The air was now simply full of barks and yelps from the dogs of every kind. Jip threw back his head and pretended to join in the chorus. But the message he shouted was directed over the wall to the Doctor:

'These idiots won't believe me. For heaven's sake tell 'em you're here – *Woof! Woof! WOO* – !'

And then still another doggish voice, coming from the garden, added to the general noise of the night. And this is what it barked:

'It is I, John Dolittle. Won't you please go away? *Wow! Woof! Wow-ow!*'

At the sound of that voice – to Blossom and Higgins no different from any of the other yelps that filled the air – the noses of all six bloodhounds left the ground and twelve long ears cocked up, motionless and listening.

'By ginger!' muttered the leader. 'It is he! It's the great man himself.'

A steeplechase over the hill and dale

'What did I tell you?' whispered Jip, shuffling towards him. 'Now lead these men off towards the south – out of the town, quick – and don't stop running till morning.'

Then the dog trainer saw his prize leader suddenly double round and head out of the passage. To his delight, the others followed his example.

'All right, Mr Blossom,' he yelled, waving his lantern. 'They've got the scent again. Come on, follow 'em, follow 'em! They're going fast. Stick to 'em! – Run!'

Tumbling over one another to keep up, the three men hurried

after the hounds; and Jip, to help the excitement in the right direction, joined the chase, barking for all he was worth.

'They've turned down the street to the south,' shouted the owner. 'We'll get your seal now, never fear. Ah, they're good dogs! Once they take a scent they never go wrong. Come on, Mr Blossom. Don't let 'em get too far away.'

And in a flash the little dark passage, which a moment before was full and crowded, was left empty in the moonlight.

Poor Sophie, weeping hysterically on the lawn, with the Doctor trying to comfort her, suddenly saw the figure of an owl pop up on to the garden wall.

'Doctor! Doctor!'

'Yes, Too-Too. What is it?'

'Now's your chance! The whole town's joined the hunt. Get your ladder. Hurry!'

And two minutes later, while the hounds, in full cry, led Blossom and Higgins on a grand steeplechase over hill and dale to the southward, the Doctor led Sophie quietly out of Ashby by the Dunwich Road, towards westward and the sea.

THE GRANTCHESTER COACH

THE night was dark without a moon that night and Sophie and John Dolittle plodded along the road between the hedgerows. Sophie's heavy and slow pace told the Doctor that even this bit of land travel was tiring the poor beast. Yet he dared not halt upon the highway.

Spying a copse over in some lonely farming lands to his left, he decided that it would make a good, snug place in which to take a rest. He therefore turned off the road, found a hole in the hedge for Sophie to crawl through and led her along a ditch that ran up towards the copse.

Arriving at the little clump of trees and brambles, they found it excellent cover and crawled in. It was the kind of place where no one would be likely to come in a month of Sundays – except perhaps stray sportsmen after rabbits, or children berry-picking.

'Well,' said the Doctor, as Sophie flopped down, panting, within the protection of dense hawthorns and furze, 'so far, so good.'

'My!' said Sophie, 'but I'm winded. Seals weren't meant for this kind of thing, Doctor. How far do you reckon we've come?'

'About a mile and a half, I should say.'

'Good Lord! Is that all? And it's nearly a hundred to the sea!'

'Don't worry,' said the Doctor with a grin. 'I have a wild idea!'

'Oh, Doctor,' sobbed Sophie, 'I'm too weary to do anything wild.' She flopped on the grass and wept.

'Now, now, Sophie,' said the Doctor, patting her on the head. 'You leave it to me. We'll rest the night here and in the morning I'll go to the near-by town and get us some food. You'll feel better.'

'That doesn't sound very wild to me,' said Sophie, sniffing only a little now. 'But I could use some food.'

'I could too,' said the Doctor. 'But I'm afraid there wouldn't be a shop open this late. Let's make the best of it and rest now.'

Next morning the cocks in the near-by farms began to crow and the Doctor set out, leaving Sophie still asleep.

After a walk of about two miles he came to a village with a pretty little ivy-covered inn, called The Three Huntsmen. Going in he ordered breakfast. He had not had anything to eat since he left the circus. A very old waiter served him some bacon and eggs in the tap-room.

As soon as the Doctor had eaten he lit his pipe and began chatting to the waiter. He found out a whole lot of things about the coaches that ran up and down the Grantchester Road – what the different ones were like to look at, at what hour they were expected, which of them were usually crowded, and much more.

Then he left the inn and walked down the street till he came to the few shops the village had. One of these was a general clothier's and haberdasher's. The Doctor entered and asked the price of a lady's cloak which was hanging in the window.

'Fifteen shillings and sixpence,' said the woman in charge of the shop. 'Is your wife tall?'

'My wife?' asked the Doctor, entirely bewildered. 'Oh, ah, yes, of course. Well – er – I want it long anyway. And I'll take a bonnet, too. And now I want a lady's veil – heavy one, please.'

'Oh, mourning in the family?'

'Er – not exactly. But I want it pretty thick – a travelling veil.'

Then the woman added a veil to the Doctor's purchases. And with a large parcel under his arm he presently left the shop. Next, he went to a grocery and bought some dried herrings for Sophie – the only kind of fish he could obtain in the village. And about noon he started back down the road.

'Sophie,' said John Dolittle, when he reached the seal's hiding-place in the woods. 'I have a whole lot of information for you, some food and some clothes.'

'Some clothes!' said Sophie. 'What would I do with clothes?'

'Wear them,' said the Doctor. 'You've got to be a lady – for a while, anyhow.'

'Great heavens!' grunted Sophie, wiping her whiskers with the back of her flipper. 'What for?'

'So as you can travel by coach,' said the Doctor.

'But I can't walk upright,' cried Sophie, 'like a lady.'

'I know. But you can sit upright – like a sick lady. You'll have to be a little lame. Any walking there is to be done, I'll carry you.'

'But what about my face? It isn't the right shape.'

'We'll cover that up with a veil,' said the Doctor, 'and your hat will disguise the rest of your head. Now, eat this fish I've brought you and then we will rehearse dressing you up.'

Then the Doctor dressed up Sophie, the performing seal, like a lady. He seated her on a log, put the bonnet on her head, the veil across her face and the cloak over the rest of her.

After he had got her into a human sitting position on the log it was surprising how natural she looked. In the deep hood of the bonnet her long nose was entirely concealed; and with the veil hung over the front of it, her head looked extraordinarily like a woman's.

He put the veil across her face

'How am I supposed to breathe?' asked Sophie, blowing out the veil in front like a balloon.

'Don't do that,' said the Doctor. 'You're not swimming or coming up for air. You'll get used to it after a while.'

'I can't keep very steady this way, Doctor. I'm sitting on the back of my spine, you know. It's an awfully hard position for balancing – much worse than walking on a ladder. What if I should slip down to the floor of the coach?'

'The seat will be wider than this log and more comfortable. Besides, I'll try to get you into a corner and I'll sit close beside you – so you'll be sort of wedged in. If you feel yourself slipping just whisper to me and I'll hitch you up into a safer position. You look splendid – really, you do.'

When evening came it found him by the edge of the road, with a heavily veiled woman seated at his side, waiting for the Grantchester coach.

THE OLD PLOUGH HORSE

AFTER they had waited about a quarter of an hour, Sophie said:

'I hear wheels, Doctor. And look, there are the lights, far down the road.'

'Ah!' said the Doctor. 'That's ours all right. Now sit up by the side of the road and keep perfectly still till I signal the driver. Then I'll lift you in, and let's hope we find a corner seat empty. Is your bonnet on tight?'

'Yes,' said Sophie, 'but the veil is tickling my nose most awfully. I do hope I don't sneeze.'

'So do I,' said the Doctor, remembering the cow-like bellow that seals make when they sneeze.

Then John Dolittle stepped out into the middle of the road and stopped the coach. Inside he found three passengers – two men at the far end and an old lady near the door. To his delight, the corner seat opposite the old lady was empty.

Leaving the door open, he ran back and got Sophie and carried her to the coach. The two men at the far end were talking earnestly together about politics. They took little notice as the lame woman was lifted in and made comfortable in the corner seat. But as the Doctor closed the door and sat beside his companion, he noticed that the old lady opposite was very interested in his invalid.

The coach started off, and the Doctor, after making sure that Sophie's flippers were not showing below the long cape, got out a newspaper from his pocket. Although the light from the oil lamp overhead was too dim to read by, he spread out the

'Excuse me, my dear,' she began

paper before his face and pretended to be deeply absorbed in it.

Presently the old lady leaned forward and tapped Sophie on the knee.

'Excuse me, my dear,' she began in a kindly voice.

'Oh, er – ' said the Doctor, looking up quickly. 'She doesn't talk – er – that is, not any English.'

'Has she got far to go?' asked the old lady.

'To Alaska,' said the Doctor, forgetting himself, 'er – that is, eventually. This journey we're only going to Grantchester.'

Wishing people would mind their own business, the Doctor

plunged again into his paper as though his life depended on his reading every word.

But the kindly passenger was not easily put off. After a moment she leaned forward once more and tapped the Doctor on the knee.

'Is it rheumatics?' she asked in a whisper, nodding towards Sophie. 'I noticed that you had to carry her in, poor dear!'

'Er, not exactly,' stammered the Doctor. 'Her legs are too short. Can't walk a step. Been that way all her life.'

'Dear me! How sad; how very sad! She'll be your daughter, I suppose?' asked the old lady.

But this time Sophie spoke for herself. A deep roar suddenly shook the carriage. The tickling of the veil had finally made her sneeze. And before the Doctor could avoid it she slid down on to the floor between his feet.

'She's in pain, poor thing,' said the old lady. 'Wait till I get my smelling-bottle. She's fainted. I often do it myself, travelling. And this coach does smell something horrible – fishy-like.'

Luckily for the Doctor, the old lady then busied herself hunting in her handbag. He was therefore able, while lifting the seal back on to the seat, to place himself in between Sophie and the two men, who were now also showing interest in her.

'Here you are,' said the old lady, handing out a smelling-bottle. 'Lift up her veil and hold it under her nose.'

'No, thank you,' said the Doctor quickly. 'All she needs is rest. She's very tired. We'll prop her snugly in the corner, like this – so. Now, let's not talk, and probably she'll drop off to sleep.'

The two men continued glancing in Sophie's direction and talking in whispers in a way that made the Doctor very uneasy.

Presently the coach stopped to change horses. The driver told the passengers that if they wished to have supper at the inn they had half an hour to do so.

The two men left the coach, eyeing Sophie and the Doctor as they passed on their way out; and soon the old lady followed their example. The driver had also disappeared and John Dolittle and his companion had the coach to themselves.

'Listen, Sophie,' the Doctor whispered, 'I'm getting worried about those two men. I'm afraid they suspect that you are not what you pretend to be. You stay here while I go in and find out if they're travelling any farther with us.'

Then he strolled into the inn. In the passage he met a serving-maid.

'Pardon me,' he began. 'Do you happen to know who those two men were who came in off the coach just now?'

'Yes, sir,' said the maid. 'One of them's the County Constable and the other's Mr Tuttle, the Mayor of Penchurch.'

'Thank you,' said the Doctor, and passed on.

Reaching the screen door, he hesitated a moment before entering the dining-room. And presently, he heard the voices of the two men seated at a table within on the other side of the screen.

'I tell you,' one said in a low tone, 'there's not the least doubt. They're highwaymen, as sure as you're alive. It's an old trick, disguising as a woman. Did you notice the thick veil? As likely as not it's that rogue, Robert Finch himself. He robbed the Twinborough Express only last month.'

'I shouldn't wonder,' said the other. 'And the short, thick villain will be Joe Gresham, his partner. Now I'll tell you what we'll do – after supper let's go back and take our seats as though we suspected nothing. Their plan, no doubt, is to wait till the coach is full and has reached a lonely part of the road. Then they'll hold up the passengers – money or your life! – and get away before the alarm can be raised. Have you got your travelling pistols?'

'Yes.'

'All right, give me one. Now, when I nudge you – you tear off the man's veil and hold a pistol to his head. I'll take care of the short one. Then we'll turn the coach about, drive back and lodge them in the village jail. Understand?'

Without waiting to have supper the Doctor left the inn and sped across the yard to the coach.

'Sophie,' he whispered, 'come out of there. They think we are highwaymen in disguise. Let's get away – quick – while the coast is clear.'

Hoisting the seal's huge weight in his arms the Doctor staggered out of the yard, across the road, and into the ditch on the other side. He put her down.

'Give me your cloak and bonnet – that's it. Now you can travel better.'

A few minutes later they were safe behind a high hedge, resting in the long grass of a meadow.

'My!' sighed Sophie, stretching herself out. 'It's good to be rid of that wretched cloak and veil. I don't like being a lady a bit. And as for coaches – I'd rather swim.'

'I'm sure you would,' said the Doctor. 'But, thank goodness, we're much farther on our way.'

'How long to the Bristol Channel now?' asked Sophie.

'Well,' began the Doctor, 'I'm not too sure, but I think about two days – walking.'

'Walking?' cried Sophie. 'I can't walk it, Doctor, I simply can't. Not two whole days.'

'S-h-h!' whispered John Dolittle. 'I think I hear something moving beyond that hedge.'

Whoever it was, he seemed determined to enter the field at that point. So with a whispered word to Sophie, the Doctor sprang up and started off, running, across the meadow, with the poor seal flopping along at his side.

On and on they went. Behind them they heard heavy footsteps beating the ground in pursuit.

Presently the Doctor, knowing that they were losing the race, turned to look back.

And there, lumbering along behind them, was an old, old plough horse!

'It's all right, Sophie,' panted the Doctor halting. 'It isn't a man at all. We've had our run for nothing. Good Lord, but I'm blown!'

The horse, seeing them stop, slowed down to a walk, and came ambling towards them in the moonlight. He seemed very decrepit and feeble; and when he came up Sophie saw with great astonishment that he was wearing spectacles.

'Heavens!' cried the Doctor. 'It's my old friend from Pud-

John Dolittle peered through them

dleby. Why didn't you call to me, instead of chasing us across country?'

'Is that John Dolittle's voice I hear?' asked the old horse, peering close into the Doctor's face.

'Yes,' said the Doctor. 'Can't you see me?'

'Only very mistily,' said the plough horse. 'My sight's been getting awful bad the last few months. I saw fine for quite a while after you gave me the spectacles. Then I got sold to another farmer, and I left Puddleby to come here. One day I fell on my nose, while ploughing and after I got up my spectacles didn't seem to work right at all. I've been almost blind ever since.'

'Let me take your glasses off and and look at them,' said the Doctor. 'Perhaps you need your prescription changed.'

Then John Dolittle took the spectacles off the old horse and, holding them up to the moon, peered through them, turning them this way and that.

'Why, good gracious!' he cried. 'You've got the lenses all twisted. No wonder you couldn't see! That right glass I gave you is quite a strong one. Most important to have them in proper adjustment. I'll soon set them right for you.'

'I did take them to the blacksmith who does my shoes,' said the old horse, as the Doctor started screwing the glasses around in the frames. 'But he only hammered the rims and made them worse than ever.'

'There, now,' said the Doctor, putting the spectacles back on his old friend's nose, 'I've fixed them tight, so they can't turn. I think you'll find them all right now.'

'Oh, my, yes,' said the old horse, a broad smile spreading over his face as he looked through them. 'I can see you as plain as day. Goodness! How natural you look – big nose, high hat and all! The sight of you does me good. Why, I can see the very blades of grass by moonlight. You've no idea what an inconvenience it is to be short-sighted, if you're a horse. You spend most of your grazing time spitting out the wild garlic that you chew by accident ... My, oh, my! You're the only animal-doctor there ever was!'

THE BRISTOL CHANNEL

'Is he a decent fellow, this farmer you're working for now?' asked the Doctor, seating himself in the grass of the meadow.

'Oh, yes,' said the old horse. 'He means well. But I haven't done much work this year. He's got a younger team for ploughing. I'm sort of pensioned off – only to odd jobs. But what's this animal you have with you,' asked the plough horse as Sophie moved restlessly in the grass, 'a badger?'

'No, that's a seal. Let me introduce you: this is Sophie, from Alaska. We're escaping from the circus. She has to go back to her country on urgent business, and I'm helping her get to the Bristol Channel. From there she can swim to the sea and a few days – at her swimming speed – should get her to Alaska in record time.'

'Perhaps I can help,' said the old horse. 'Listen; you see that barn up on the skyline? Well, there's an old wagon in it. There's no harness but there's plenty of ropes. Let's run up there, and you can hitch me between the shafts, put your seal in the wagon and we'll go.'

'But you'll get into trouble,' said the Doctor, 'taking your farmer's wagon off like that.'

'My farmer will never know,' said the old horse, grinning behind his spectacles. 'You leave the gate on the latch as we go out and I'll bring the wagon back and put it where we found it.'

'But how will you get out of your harness alone?'

'That's easy. If you knot the ropes the way I tell you, I can undo them with my teeth. I won't be able to take you the whole way, because I couldn't get back in time to put the wagon away before daylight comes. But I've got a friend about nine miles down the Grantchester Road, on the Redhill Farm. He gets put out to graze nights, like me. He'll take you the rest of the way. It'll be easy for him to get back to his place before anyone's about.'

'Old friend,' said the Doctor, 'you have a great head. Let's hurry and get on our way.'

They climbed the hill to the barn. John Dolittle hitched up the horse, being careful to make all the knots exactly the way he was told. Then lifting Sophie into the wagon they started off down the meadow towards the gate. As they were driving out the Doctor said:

'But suppose any one should meet me driving a wagon in a high hat? Wouldn't it seem sort of suspicious? Oh, look: there's a scarecrow in the next field. I'll borrow his hat.'

'Bring the whole scarecrow with you,' the old horse called after him as the Doctor started off. 'I'll need something as a dummy driver when I'm coming back. Folks would stop me if they thought I was straying around the country without a driver.'

'All right,' said the Doctor and he ran off.

In a few minutes he came marching back with the scarecrow on his shoulder. Then he set the gate on the latch, so the old horse could push it open on his return, threw the scarecrow up into the wagon and climbed in himself.

Next, he took the scarecrow's tattered hat and put it on his own head, in place of his high one. Then he got into the driving seat, lifted the rope reins in his hands, called 'Gee-up!' to his old friend between the shafts and they started off.

'You'd better keep your cloak and bonnet ready to slip on, Sophie,' said he. 'Somebody might ask for a ride. And if we are compelled to give anyone a lift you'll have to be a lady again.'

'I'd sooner be almost anything in the world than a lady,' sighed Sophie, remembering the tickling veil. 'But I'll do it if you say so.'

Thus, driving his own farm-wagon coach, with a scarecrow and a seal for passengers, John Dolittle successfully completed the next stage of his strange journey. They passed very few people, and no one asked for a ride.

A little farther on the plough horse stopped.

'This is Redhill Farm on the right,' said he. 'Wait till I call Joe.'

Then he went close to the hedge beside the road and neighed softly. Presently there was a scampering of hoofs and his friend, a much younger horse, poked his head over the hawthorns.

'I've got John Dolittle here,' whispered the plough horse. 'He wants to get to the Bristol Channel in a hurry. Can you take him?'

'Why, certainly,' said the other.

'You'll have to use a wagon of your own,' said the plough horse. 'I must get mine back to the barn before my farmer wakes up. Got a cart or something anywhere about the place?'

'Yes, there's a trap up in the yard. It'll be faster than a wagon. Come over this side of the hedge, Doctor, and I'll show you where it is.'

Then, hurrying lest daylight overtake them, they made the exchange. Madame Sophie was transferred from a farm wagon to a smart trap. The old plough horse, after an affectionate farewell from the Doctor, started back with his own wagon, driven by his scarecrow propped up on the front seat. At the same time John Dolittle and Sophie were carried at a good, swift pace in the opposite direction, towards the Channel.

John Dolittle and Sophie now found that the worst part of their troublesome travelling was over.

Gradually the landscape changed to a kind of scenery which, so far, they had not met with on their journey. They began to see the lights of the seaport town twinkling in the distance. The land sloped upward to the cliffs overlooking the Bristol Channel.

Not wanting to involve the Redhill horse in what might still be a dangerous venture, the Doctor drew up the reins and lifted Sophie down from the trap.

'Thank you for your kindness,' he said to the horse. 'We had better go on foot from here. You will just have time enough to return without being missed.'

'Not at all,' replied the Redhill horse. 'It was my proud pleasure to assist you, Doctor Dolittle. Good-bye!'

The Doctor made Sophie keep her bonnet on, and he had her cloak ready to throw over her at any minute, because there were many roads to cross and farmhouses to pass upon the way.

About a mile had to be covered before they would reach the top of the long slope and come in sight of the sea beyond the cliffs. Picking out a line which would miss most of the barns on the downs, they proceeded steadily and slowly forward. On this upland country they met with many stone walls. And, though they were low enough for the Doctor to jump, they were too much for Sophie to manage and the Doctor had to lift her over.

She did not complain, but the uphill going was telling on her terribly. And when at last they came to a level stretch at the top,

He threw Sophie into the Bristol Channel

and the wind from the Channel beat in their faces, Sophie was absolutely exhausted and unable to walk another step.

The distance now remaining to the edge of the cliffs was not more than a hundred yards. Hearing the voices of people singing in a house near by, the Doctor began to fear that they might yet be discovered – even with the end of their long trip in sight. So, with poor Sophie in a state of utter collapse, he decided there was nothing for it but to carry her the remainder of the journey.

As he put the cloak about her he saw the door of the house open and two men come out. Hurriedly he caught the seal up in his arms and staggered with her towards the edge of the cliffs.

'Oh,' cried Sophie when they had gone a few yards, 'look, the sea! How fresh and nice it sparkles in the moonlight. The sea, at last!'

'Yes, this is the end of your troubles, Sophie,' the Doctor panted as he stumbled forward. 'Give my regards to the herd when you reach Alaska.'

At the edge John Dolittle looked straight downward to where the deep salt water swirled and eddied far below.

'Good-bye, Sophie!' he said with what breath he had left. 'Good-bye, and good luck!'

Then, with a last tremendous effort, he threw Sophie over the cliff into the Bristol Channel.

Turning and twisting in the air, the seal sped downward – her cloak and bonnet, torn off her by the rushing air, floating more slowly behind. And as she landed in the water the Doctor saw the white foam break over her and the noise of a splash gently reached his ears.

'Well,' he said, mopping his brow with a handkerchief, 'thank goodness for that! We did it, after all. I can tell Matthew that Sophie reached the sea.'

NIGHTSHADE, THE VIXEN

AFTER helping Sophie the seal to escape, the Doctor decided he would walk back to the circus. It wasn't so much a matter of choice; he discovered that he hadn't enough money to take the coach.

'Let's see,' he muttered, counting the few coins in his hand. 'That's only enough to take me a few miles. I'd better walk.'

When he reached the town of Appledyke he bought a loaf of bread, tucked it under his arm and set off across the country.

Soon he decided it was lunch-time and looked about him for a brook where he might get a drink of clean water to wash down his dry-bread meal. Over to his right he saw a place where the land dipped downwards into a hollow filled with trees and bushes.

'I'll bet there's a brook down there,' the Doctor murmured. 'It is certainly most delightful country, this.'

Then he climbed over a stile and set off across the meadows which led down into the hollow.

He found his brook all right; and the banks of it, shaded by the trees, formed the most charming picnicking ground anyone could wish for.

After his lunch the Doctor felt that before going on with his journey he would like to rest a while in this pleasant spot. So he leaned back against the trunk of the oak tree and soon he fell asleep to the music of the murmuring brook.

When he awoke he found four foxes, a vixen with three cubs, sitting patiently beside him waiting till he should finish his nap.

'Good afternoon,' said the vixen. 'My name is Nightshade. Of course, I've heard a lot about you. But I had no idea you were in the district. I've often thought of coming all the way to Puddleby to see you. I'm awfully glad I didn't miss you on this visit. A starling told me you were here.'

'Well,' said the Doctor, sitting up, 'I'm glad to see you. What can I do for you?'

'One of these children of mine,' the vixen pointed towards her three round little cubs who were gazing at the famous Doctor in great awe, 'one of these children has something wrong with his front paws. I wish you would take a look at him.'

'Certainly,' said the Doctor. 'Come here, young fellow.'

'He has never been able to run properly,' said the mother as John Dolittle took the cub on his lap and examined him. 'It has nearly cost us all our lives, his slow pace, when the dogs have been after us. The others can run beautifully. Can you tell me what's the matter with him?'

'Why, of course,' said the Doctor, who now had the cub upside down on his knees with its four big paws waving in the air. 'It's a case of flat feet. That's all. The muscles of the pads are weak. He can get no grip of the ground without good pad

'It's a case of flat feet'

muscles. you'll have to exercise him morning and night. Make him rise on his toes like this: One, two! One, two! One, two!'

And the Doctor stood up and gave a demonstration of the exercise which in a person strengthens the arches of the feet and in a fox develops the muscles of the paw pads.

'If you make him do that twenty or thirty times every morning and every night I think you'll soon find his speed will get better,' said the Doctor.

'Thank you very much,' said the vixen. 'I have the greatest

difficulty making my children do anything regularly. Now you hear what the Doctor says, Dandelion; every morning and every night, thirty times, up on your toes as high as you can go. I don't want any flat-footed cubs in my family. We've always been – great heavens! Listen!'

The mother fox had stopped speaking, the beautiful brush of her tail straight and quivering, her nose outstretched, pitiful terror staring from her wide-open eyes. And in the little silence that followed, from over the rising ground away off to the north-eastward, came the dread sound that makes every fox's heart stand still.

'*The horn!*' she whispered through chattering teeth. 'They're out! It's th – th – the huntsman's horn!'

As he looked at the trembling creature John Dolittle was reminded of the occasion which had made him an enemy of fox-hunting for life – when he had met an old dog fox one evening lying half dead with exhaustion under a tangle of blackberries.

As the horn rang out again the poor vixen began running round her cubs like a crazy thing.

'Oh, what *shall* I do?' she moaned. 'The children! If it wasn't for them I could perhaps give the dogs the slip. Oh, why did I bring them out in daylight to see you? I suppose I was afraid you might be gone if I waited till after dark. Now I've left our scent behind us, all the way from Broad Meadows, as plain as the nose on your face. And I've come right into the wind. What a fool I was! What shall I do? What shall I do?'

As the horn sounded the third time, louder and nearer, joined by the yelping of hounds in full cry, the little cubs scuttled to their mother and cowered under her.

A very firm look came into the Doctor's face.

'What pack is this?' he asked. 'Do you know the name of it?'

'It's probably the Ditcham – their kennels are just the other side of Hallam's Acre. It might be the Wiltborough, over from Buckley Downs – they sometimes hunt this way. But most likely it's the Ditcham – the best pack in these parts. They were after me last week. But my sister crossed my trail just below Fenton Ridge and they went after her – and got her. There's the horn again! Oh, what a fool I was to bring these children out in daylight!'

'Don't worry, Nightshade,' said the Doctor. 'Even if it's the Ditcham and the Wiltborough together, they're not going to get you today – nor your children either. Let the cubs get into my pockets – come on, hop in, young fellows – so. Now you, Nightshade, come inside the breast of my coat. That's the way – get farther round towards the back. And you can stick your feet and your brush into the tail-pocket. And when I've buttoned it up like this – see? – you will be completely covered. Can you breathe all right back there?'

'Yes, I can breathe,' said the vixen. 'But it won't do us much good to be out of sight. The hounds can smell us – that's the way they run us down – with their noses.'

'Yes, I know,' said the Doctor. 'But the men can't smell you. I can deal with the dogs all right. But you mustn't be seen by the men. Keep as still as a stone, all four of you – don't move or try to run for it, whatever happens.'

And then John Dolittle, with his coat bulging with foxes in all directions, stood in a little clearing in the wooded hollow and awaited the oncoming of the Ditcham hunt in full cry.

The mingled noises of the dogs, men, horns and horses grew louder. And soon, peeping through the crossing branches of his cover, the Doctor saw the first hounds come in view at the top of the ridge.

Ahead of most of the huntsmen galloped one man, old, lean and white-haired – Sir William Peabody, the Master of the Foxhounds. Halfway down the slope he turned in his saddle and called to a man on a grey mare close behind him.

'Jones, they're making for the spinney. Don't let the leaders break into it before we've got it surrounded. Watch Galloway; he's rods ahead. Mind he doesn't put the fox out the other side. Watch Galloway!'

Then the man on the grey mare spurted ahead, cracking a long whip and calling, 'Galloway! Here, Galloway!'

As the Doctor peered through the foliage he saw that the leading hound was now quite close. But, wonderfully trained to the huntsmen's command, Galloway suddenly slacked his pace within a few yards of the trees and remained, yelping and barking, for the others to come up.

'My goodness!' murmured the Doctor. 'Was there ever anything so childish? All this fuss for a poor little fox!'

As the hounds, under the guidance of the men with long whips, spread, yelping, around all sides of the spinney, the people called and shouted to one another and the noise was tremendous.

'We'll get him,' bellowed a fat farmer on a pony. 'It's a killing, sure. Wait till Jones lets 'em into the spinney. We'll get him!'

'Oh, no, you won't,' the Doctor muttered, the firm look coming back into his face. 'Not today, my fat friend – not today.'

The dogs, impatient and eager, sniffed and ran hither and thither, waiting for permission to enter the little patch of woods and finish the hunt.

Suddenly a command was given and instantly they leapt the underbrush from all sides.

John Dolittle was standing in his clearing, with his hands over his pockets, trying to look all ways at once at the moment when the hounds broke in. Suddenly, before he knew it, four heavy dogs had leapt on his back, and he went down on the ground, simply smothered under a tangled pile of yelping, fighting foxhounds.

Kicking and punching in all directions, the Doctor struggled to his feet.

'Get away!' he said in dog language. 'Lead the hunt somewhere else. This fox is mine.'

The hounds, spoken to in their own tongue, now had no doubt as to who the little man was that they had knocked down.

'I'm awfully sorry,' Doctor,' said Galloway, a fine, deep-chested dog, with a tan patch over one eye. 'We had no idea it was you. We jumped on you from behind, you know. Why didn't you call to us while we were outside?'

'How could I?' said the Doctor irritably, pushing away a dog who was sniffing at his pocket. 'How could I – with you duffers making all that din? Look out, here come the huntsmen. Don't let them see you smelling around me. Get the pack out of here, Galloway, quick.'

'All right, Doctor. But it smells to me as though you had more than one fox in your pockets,' said Galloway.

'I've got a whole family,' said the Doctor. 'And I mean to keep them, too.'

'Can't you let us have even one of them, Doctor?' asked the hound. 'They're sneaky little things. They eat rabbits and chickens, you know.'

'No,' said the Doctor, 'I can't. They have to get food for themselves. You have food given to you. Go away – and hurry about it.'

At that moment Sir William Peabody came up.

'Great heavens! Dolittle!' he exclaimed. 'Did you see the fox? Hounds headed right down into this hollow.'

'I wouldn't tell you, Will, if I had seen him,' said the Doctor. 'You know what I think of fox-hunting.'

'Funny thing!' muttered Sir William as he watched the dogs lurching among the brush uncertainly. 'They can't have lost the scent, surely. They came down here as firm as you like. Curious!'

At that moment a cry came from the huntsmen that the hounds had found another scent and were going off to the southward. Sir William, who had dismounted, ran for his horse.

'Hang you, Dolittle!' he shouted. 'You've led the hounds astray.'

The few dogs remaining within the spinney were now melting away like shadows. One of the fox cubs stirred in the Doctor's pocket. Sir William had already mounted his horse outside.

'Goodness, I forgot!' muttered the Doctor. 'I must ask Will for a guinea – I say, Will!'

Then John Dolittle, his pockets full of foxes, ran out of the spinney after the Master of the Hunt.

'Listen, Will!' he called. 'Would you lend me a guinea? I haven't any money to get to Ashby with.'

Sir William turned in his saddle and drew rein.

'I'll lend you five guineas – or ten – John,' said Sir William, 'if you'll only get out of this district and stop putting my hounds on false scents. Here you are.'

'Thanks, Will,' said the Doctor, taking the money and dropping it in his pocket on top of one of the cubs. 'I'll send it back to you by mail.'

Then he stood there by the edge of the spinney and watched the huntsmen, hallooing and galloping, disappear over the skyline to the southward.

'What a childish sport!' he murmured. 'I can't understand what they see in it. Really, I can't. Grown men rushing about the landscape on horseback, caterwauling and blowing tin horns – all after one poor little wild animal! Perfectly childish!'

Returning to the side of the brook within the shelter of the trees, the Doctor took the foxes out of his pockets and set them on the ground.

'Be careful now, Nightshade,' he said. 'And don't take any more chances.' He leant over and patted Dandelion, the flat-footed cub, on the head. 'And you, little fellow – up and down on the toes. Don't forget.'

'Thank you, John Dolittle,' said the vixen as she trotted off with her family to their lair. 'We owe our lives to you. And I'll never forget it. Good-bye.'

And now, with Sophie safely on her way to Alaska to rejoin her husband, Slushy, and Nightshade and her cubs out of danger for the moment from the hounds. Doctor Dolittle set off to find a coach to carry him back in the direction of Ashby.

Many months later he was to return to Puddleby-on-the-Marsh. But not before many adventures had befallen him. The first – and most surprising – was how he came to own and operate the circus.

One day, after a long series of successful performances in which the Doctor's animal family and friends had made the

Putting up the new sign

Blossom Circus a smashing success, Jip came running to the Doctor's wagon and joined the animals there.

'Fellows,' he said, 'Alexander Blossom has skedaddled!'

'Good heavens!' cried Too-Too. 'With the money?'

'Yes, with the money – drat him!' growled Jip. 'And there was enough coming to the Doctor to keep us in comfort for the rest of our days.'

'I knew it!' groaned Dab-Dab, throwing out her wing in despair. 'I told the Doctor not to trust him. I guessed him to be a fishy customer from the start. Now he's wallowing in luxury while we scrape and pinch to pay the bills he left behind.'

'Oh, what does it matter?' cried Gub-Gub. 'So much the better if he's gone. Now we'll have a real circus – The Dolittle Circus – which the animals have hoped for. Good riddance to Blossom – the crook! I'm glad he's gone.'

Well, the Doctor *did* take over the circus. And with such success that when he was ready to return to Puddleby he had enough money to send all the jungle animals – by special boat – back to their home countries.

Each act was given a share of the profits – even the animals like Jip, Gub-Gub, Dab-Dab, the white mouse, Swizzle the clown's dog and Toby the Punch-and-Judy dog were given their own bank accounts.

One day before the Doctor announced he would leave, a vast throng of youngsters came with an enormous bouquet of flowers, to bid him good-bye. And this, when he walked down the steps of his wagon, was (he told Matthew Mugg afterwards, when they were on the road to Puddleby) the only thing that made him feel sorry at leaving the life of the circus behind.

The VOYAGES of
DOCTOR DOLITTLE
ILLUSTRATED BY THE AUTHOR
BY HUGH LOFTING

THE COBBLER'S SON

FIRST of all I must tell you something about myself. My name is Tommy Stubbins, son of Jacob Stubbins, the cobbler of Puddleby-on-the-Marsh; and I was nine and a half years old when I first met the famous Doctor Dolittle.

At that time Puddleby was only quite a small town. A river ran through the middle of it; and over this river there was a very old stone bridge, called Kingsbridge.

Sailing-ships came up this river from the sea and anchored near the bridge. I would sit on the river-wall with my feet dangling over the water and watch the sailors unloading the ships and listen to their songs until I too could sing them by heart.

When they set sail again I longed to go with them and would sit dreaming of the wonderful lands I had never seen.

Three great friends I had in Puddleby in those days. One was Joe, the mussel-man, who lived in a tiny hut by the edge of the water under the bridge. This old man was simply marvellous at making things. I never saw a man so clever with his hands. He used to mend my toy ships for me which I sailed upon the river; he built windmills out of packing-cases and barrel-staves; and he could make the most wonderful kites from old umbrellas.

Another friend I had was Matthew Mugg, the Cat's-meat-Man. He was a funny old person with a bad squint. He looked rather awful but he was really quite nice to talk to. He knew everybody in Puddleby; and he knew all the dogs and all the cats. In those times being a Cat's-meat-Man was a regular business. And you could see one nearly any day going through the streets with a wooden tray full of pieces of meat stuck on skewers and crying, 'Meat! M–E–A–T!' People paid him to give this meat to

I would sit on the river-wall with my feet dangling over the water their cats and dogs instead of feeding them on dog-biscuits or the scraps from the table.

My third great friend was Luke the Hermit. But of him I will tell you more later on.

I did not go to school; because my father was not rich enough to send me. But I was extremely fond of animals. So I used to spend my time collecting birds' eggs and butterflies, fishing in the river, rambling through the countryside after blackberries and mushrooms and helping the mussel-man mend his nets.

One early morning in the springtime, when I was wandering among the hills at the back of the town, I happened to come upon a hawk with a squirrel in its claws. It was standing on a rock and the squirrel was fighting very hard for its life. The hawk was so frightened when I came upon it suddenly like this that it dropped the poor creature and flew away. I picked the squirrel up and found that two of its legs were badly hurt. So I carried it in my arms back to the town.

When I came to the bridge I went into the mussel-man's hut and asked him if he could do anything for it, Joe put on his spectacles and examined it carefully. Then he shook his head.

'Yon crittur's got a broken leg,' he said, 'and another badly cut an' all. I can mend your boats, Tom, but I haven't the tools nor the learning to make a broken squirrel seaworthy. This is a job for a surgeon – and for a right smart one an' all. There be only one man I know who could save yon crittur's life. And that's John Dolittle.'

'Who is John Dolittle?' I asked. 'Is he a vet?'

'No,' said the mussel-man, 'he's no vet. Doctor Dolittle is a nacheralist.'

'What's a nacheralist?'

'A nacheralist,' said Joe, putting away his glasses and starting to fill his pipe, "is a man who knows all about animals and butterflies and plants and rocks an' all. John Dolittle is a very great nacheralist. I'm surprised you never heard of him – and you daft over animals. He knows a lot about shellfish – that I know from my own knowledge. He's a quiet man and don't talk much; but there's folks who do say he's the greatest nacheralist in the world.'

'Where does he live?' I asked.

'Over on the Oxenthorpe Road, t'other side the town. Don't know just which house it is, but 'most anyone 'cross there could tell you, I reckon. Go and see him. He's a great man.'

So I thanked the mussel-man, took up my squirrel again and started off towards the Oxenthorpe Road.

The first thing I heard as I came into the market-place was someone calling, 'Meat! M–E–A–T!'

'There's Matthew Mugg,' I said to myself. 'He'll know where this Doctor lives. Matthew knows everyone.'

So I hurried across the market-place and caught him up.

'Matthew,' I said, 'do you know Doctor Dolittle?'

'Do I know John Dolittle!' said he. 'Well, I should think I do! I know him as well as I know my own wife – better, I sometimes think. He's a great man – a very great man.'

'Can you show me where he lives?' I asked. 'I want to take this squirrel to him. It has a broken leg.'

'Certainly,' said the Cat's-meat-Man. 'I'll be going right by his house directly. Come along and I'll show you.'

So off we went together.

'Oh, I've known John Dolittle for years and years,' said Matthew as we made our way out of the market-place. 'But I'm pretty sure he ain't home just now. He's away on a voyage. But he's liable to be back any day. I'll show you his house and then you'll know where to find him.'

All the way down the Oxenthorpe Road Matthew hardly stopped talking about his great friend, Doctor John Dolittle – 'M.D.'. He talked so much that he forgot all about calling out 'Meat!' until we both suddenly noticed that we had a whole procession of dogs following us patiently.

'Where did the Doctor go to on this voyage?' I asked as Matthew handed round the meat to them.

'I couldn't tell you,' he answered. 'Nobody never knows where he goes, nor when he's going, nor when he's coming back. He lives all alone except for his pets. He's made some great voyages and some wonderful discoveries. And as for animals, well, there ain't no one knows as much about 'em as what he does.'

'How did he get to know so much about animals?' I asked.

The Cat's-meat-Man stopped and leant down to whisper in my ear.

'*He talks their language*,' he said in a hoarse, mysterious voice.

'The animals' language?' I cried.

'Why certainly,' said Matthew. 'All animals have some kind of a language. Some sorts talk more than others; some only speak in sign-language, like deaf-and-dumb. But the Doctor, he understands them all – birds as well as animals. We keep it a secret though, him and me, because folks only laugh at you when you speak of it. Why, he can even write animal-language. He reads aloud to his pets. He's wrote history-books in monkey-talk, poetry in canary-language and comic songs for magpies to sing. It's a fact. He's now busy learning the language of the shellfish. But he says it's hard work – and he has caught some terrible colds, holding his head under water so much. He's a great man.'

'He certainly must be,' I said. 'I do wish he were home so I could meet him.'

'Well, there's his house, look,' said the Cat's-meat-Man. 'That little one at the bend in the road there – the one high up – like it was sitting on the wall above the street.'

We were now come beyond the edge of the town. And the house that Matthew pointed out was quite a small one standing by itself. There seemed to be a big garden around it; and this garden was much higher than the road, so you had to go up a flight of steps in the wall before you reached the front gate at the top.

When we reached the house Matthew went up the steps and I followed him. I thought he was going to go into the garden; but the gate was locked. A dog came running down from the house; and he took several pieces of meat which the Cat's-meat-Man pushed through the bars of the gate, and some paper bags full of corn and bran. I noticed that this dog did not stop to eat the meat, as any ordinary dog would have done, but he took all the things back to the house and disappeared. He had a curious wide collar round his neck which looked as though it were made of brass or something. Then we came away.

'The Doctor isn't back yet,' said Matthew, 'or the gate wouldn't be locked.'

'What were all those things in paper bags you gave the dog?' I asked.

'Oh, those were provisions,' said Matthew; 'things for the animals to eat. The Doctor's house is simply full of pets. I give the things to the dog, while the Doctor's away, and the dog gives them to the other animals.'

'And what was that curious collar he was wearing round his neck?'

'That's a solid gold dog-collar,' said Matthew. 'It was given to him when he was with the Doctor on one of his voyages long ago. He saved a man's life.'

'How long has the Doctor had him?' I asked.

'Oh, a long time. Jip's getting pretty old now. That's why the Doctor doesn't take him on his voyages any more. He leaves him behind to take care of the house. Every Monday and Thursday I bring the food to the gate here and give it to him through the bars. He never lets any one come inside the garden while the Doctor's away – not even me, though he knows me well. But you'll be able to tell if the Doctor's back or not – because if he is, the gate will surely be open.'

So I went off home to my father's house and put my squirrel to bed in an old wooden box full of straw. And there I nursed him myself and took care of him as best I could till the time should come when the Doctor would return. And every day I went to the little house with the big garden on the edge of the town and tried to see if it were locked. Sometimes the dog, Jip, would come down to the gate to meet me. But though he always wagged his tail and seemed glad to see me, he never let me come inside the garden.

THE DOCTOR'S HOUSE

ONE afternoon, about a week later, my father asked me to take some shoes which he had mended to a house on the other side of town. After I had delivered the shoes I thought I'd just like to go and take another look and see if the Doctor had returned yet. My squirrel wasn't getting any better and I was beginning to be worried about him.

I turned into the Oxenthorpe Road and started off towards the Doctor's house. On the way I noticed that the sky was clouding over and that it looked as though it might rain.

I reached the gate and found it still locked. I felt discouraged. The dog, Jip, came to the gate and watched me closely to see that I didn't get in.

I began to fear that my squirrel would die before the Doctor came back. I turned away sadly, went down the steps on to the road and turned towards home again. All of a sudden the rain came down in torrents.

I have never seen it rain so hard. It got dark, almost like night. The wind began to blow; the thunder rolled; the lightning flashed, and in a moment the gutters of the road were flowing like a river. There was no place handy to take shelter, so I put my head down against the driving wind and started to run towards home.

I hadn't gone very far when my head bumped into something soft and I sat down suddenly on the pavement. I looked up to see whom I had run into. And there in front of me, sitting on the wet pavement like myself, was a little round man with a very kind face. He wore a shabby high hat and in his hand he had a small black bag.

'I'm very sorry,' I said. 'I had my head down and I didn't see you coming.'

To my great surprise, instead of getting angry at being knocked down, the little man began to laugh.

'You know this reminds me,' he said, 'of a time once when I

'I'm very sorry,' I said

was in India. I ran full tilt into a woman in a thunderstorm. But she was carrying a pitcher of molasses on her head and I had treacle in my hair for weeks afterwards – the flies followed me everywhere. I didn't hurt you, did I?'

'No,' I said. 'I'm all right.'

'It was just as much my fault as it was yours, you know,' said the little man. 'I had my head down too – but look here, we mustn't sit talking like this. You must be soaked. I know I am. How far have you got to go?'

'My home is on the other side of the town,' I said, as we picked ourselves up.

'My goodness, but that was a wet pavement!' said he. 'And I declare it's coming down worse than ever. Come along to my house and get dried. A storm like this can't last.'

He took hold of my hand and we started running back down the road together. As we ran I began to wonder who this funny little man could be, and where he lived. I was a perfect stranger to him, and yet he was taking me to his own home to get dried.

'Here we are,' he said.

I looked up to see where we were and found myself back at the foot of the steps leading to the little house with the big garden! My new friend was already running up the steps and opening the gate with some keys he took from his pocket.

'Surely,' I thought, 'this cannot be the great Doctor Dolittle himself!'

I suppose after hearing so much about him I had expected someone very tall and strong and marvellous. It was hard to believe that this funny little man with the kind smiling face could be really he. Yet here he was, sure enough, running up the steps and opening the very gate which I had been watching for so many days!

The dog, Jip, came rushing out and started jumping up on him and barking with happiness. The rain was splashing down heavier than ever.

'Are you Doctor Dolittle?' I shouted as we sped up the short garden-path to the house.

'Yes, I'm Doctor Dolittle,' said he, opening the front door with the same bunch of keys. 'Get in! Don't bother about wiping your feet. Never mind the mud. Take it in with you. Get in out of the rain!'

I popped in, he and Jip following. Then he slammed the door to behind us.

The storm had made it dark enough outside; but inside the house, with the door closed, it was as black as night. Then began the most extraordinary noise that I have ever heard. It sounded like all sorts and kinds of animals and birds calling and squeaking and screeching at the same time. I could hear things trundling down the stairs and hurrying along passages. Somewhere in the dark a duck was quacking, a cock was crowing, a dove was cooing, an owl was hooting, a lamb was bleating, and Jip was barking. I felt birds' wings fluttering and fanning near my face. Things kept bumping into my legs and nearly upsetting me. The whole front hall seemed to be filling up with animals. The noise, together with the roaring of the rain, was tremendous; and I was beginning to grow a little bit scared when I felt the Doctor take told of my arm and shout into my ear.

'Don't be alarmed. Don't be frightened. These are just some of my pets. I've been away three months and they are glad to see me home again. Stand still where you are till I strike a light. My gracious, what a storm! – Just listen to that thunder!'

So there I stood in the pitch-black dark, while all kinds of animals which I couldn't see chattered and jostled around me. It was a curious and a funny feeling. I had often wondered, when I had looked in from the front gate, what Doctor Dolittle would be like and what the funny little house would have inside it. But I never imagined it would be anything like this. Yet somehow after I had felt the Doctor's hand upon my arm I was not frightened, only confused. It all seemed like some queer dream; and I was beginning to wonder if I was really awake, when I heard the Doctor speaking again:

'My blessed matches are all wet. They won't strike. Have you got any?'

'No, I'm afraid I haven't,' I called back.

'Never mind,' said he. 'Perhaps Dab-Dab can raise us a light somewhere.'

Then the Doctor made some funny clicking noises with his tongue and I heard someone trundle up the stairs again and start moving about in the rooms above.

Then we waited quite a while without anything happening.

'Will the light be long in coming?' I asked. 'Some animal is sitting on my foot and my toes are going to sleep.'

'No, only a minute,' said the Doctor. 'She'll be back in a minute.'

And just then I saw the first glimmerings of a light around the landing above. At once all the animals kept quiet.

'I thought you lived alone,' I said to the Doctor.

'So I do,' said he. 'It is Dab-Dab who is bringing the light.'

I looked up the stairs trying to make out who was coming. I could not see around the landing but I heard the most curious footstep on the upper flight. It sounded like someone hopping down from one step to the other, as though he were using only one leg.

As the light came lower, it grew brighter and began to throw strange jumping shadows on the walls.

'Ah – at last!' said the Doctor. 'Good old Dab-Dab!'

And then I thought I really must be dreaming. For there, craning her neck round the bend of the landing, hopping down the stairs on one leg, came a spotless white duck. And in her right foot she carried a lighted candle!

THE DOCTOR'S KITCHEN

WHEN at last I could look around me I found that the hall was indeed simply full of animals. It seemed to me that almost every kind of creature from the countryside must be there: a pigeon, a white mouse, an owl, a badger, a jackdaw – there was even a small pig, just in from the rainy garden, carefully wiping his feet on the mat while the light from the candle glistened on his wet pink back.

The Doctor took the candlestick from the duck and turned to me.

'Look here,' he said, 'you must get those wet clothes off – by the way, what is your name?'

'Tommy Stubbins,' I said.

'Oh, are you the son of Jacob Stubbins, the shoemaker?'

'Yes,' I said.

'Excellent bootmaker, your father,' said the Doctor. 'You see these?' and he held up his right foot to show me the enormous

And in her right foot she carried a lighted candle!

boots he was wearing. 'Your father made those boots four years ago, and I've been wearing them ever since – perfectly wonderful boots. Well now, look here, Stubbins. You've got to change those wet things – and quick. Wait a moment till I get some more candles lit, and then we'll go upstairs and find some dry clothes. You'll have to wear an old suit of mine till we can get yours dry again by the kitchen fire.'

We changed to two suits of the Doctor's and as soon as we had a huge fire blazing up the chimney we hung our wet clothes around on chairs.

'You'll stay and have supper with me, Stubbins, of course?'

Already I was beginning to be very fond of this funny little man who called me 'Stubbins', instead of 'Tommy' or 'little lad' (I did so hate to be called 'little lad'!) This man seemed to begin right away treating me as though I were a grown-up friend of his. And when he asked me to stop and have supper with him I felt terribly proud and happy.

'Thank you very much. I would like to stay,' I replied.

'Did you see where I put my bag?' asked the Doctor.

'I think it is still in the hall,' I said. 'I'll go and see.'

I found the bag near the front door. It was made of black leather and looked very, very old. One of its latches was broken and it was tied up round the middle with a piece of string.

'Thank you,' said the Doctor when I brought it to him.

'Was that bag all the luggage you had for your voyage?' I asked.

'Yes,' said the Doctor, as he undid the piece of string. 'I don't believe in a lot of baggage. It's such a nuisance. Life's too short to fuss with it. And it isn't really necessary, you know. Where *did* I put those sausages?'

The Doctor was feeling about inside the bag. First he brought out a loaf of new bread. Next came a glass jar of marmalade which he set upon the table. At last the Doctor brought out a pound of sausages.

'Now,' he said, 'all we want is a frying-pan.'

We went into the scullery and there we found some pots and pans hanging against the wall. The Doctor took down the

'Where *did* I put those sausages?'

frying-pan and in a few moments the sausages were sending a beautiful smell all through the room.

'Ah,' said the Doctor. 'The sausages are done to a turn. Come along – hold your plate near and let me give you some.'

Then we sat down at the kitchen table and started a hearty meal. It was a wonderful kitchen, that. I had many meals there afterwards and I found it a better place to eat in than the grandest dining-room in the world. It was so cosy and home-like and warm. It was so handy for the food too. You took it right off the fire hot, and put it on the table and ate it. And you could watch your toast toasting at the fender and see it didn't burn while you drank your soup. And if you had forgotten to put the salt on the table, you didn't have to get up and go into another room to fetch it; you just reached round and took the big wooden box off the dresser behind you. Then the fireplace – the biggest fireplace you ever saw – was like a room in itself. You could get right inside it even when the logs were burning and sit on the wide seats either side and roast chestnuts after the meal was over – or listen to the kettle singing, or tell stories, or look at picturebooks by the light of the fire. It was a marvellous kitchen. It was like the Doctor, comfortable, sensible, friendly and solid.

While we were gobbling away, the door suddenly opened and in marched the duck, Dab-Dab, and the dog, Jip, dragging sheets and pillowcases behind them over the clean tiled floor. The Doctor, seeing how surprised I was, explained:

'They're just going to air the bedding for me in front of the fire. Dab-Dab is a perfect treasure of a housekeeper; she never forgets anything. I had a sister once who used to keep house for me (poor dear Sarah! I wonder how she's getting on – I haven't seen her for many years). But she wasn't nearly as good as Dab-Dab. Have another sausage?'

The Doctor turned and said a few words to the dog and duck in some strange talk and signs. They seemed to understand him perfectly.

'Can you talk in squirrel-language?' I asked.

'Oh, yes. That's quite an easy language,' said the Doctor. 'You could learn that yourself without a great deal of trouble. But why do you ask?'

'Because I have a sick squirrel at home,' I said. 'I took it away from a hawk. But one of its legs is badly hurt and I wanted very much to have you see it, if you would. Shall I bring it tomorrow?'

'Well, if its leg is badly broken I think I had better see it tonight. It may be too late to do much; but I'll come home with you and take a look at it.'

So presently we felt the clothes by the fire and mine were found to be quite dry. I took them upstairs to the bedroom and changed, and when I came down the Doctor was all ready waiting for me with his little black bag full of medicines and bandages.

'Come along,' he said. 'The rain has stopped now.'

Outside it had grown bright again and the evening sky was all red with the setting sun; and thrushes were singing in the garden as we opened the gate to go down on to the road.

POLYNESIA

'It must be splendid,' I said, as we set off in the direction of my home, 'to be able to talk all the languages of the different animals. Do you think I could ever learn to do it?'

'Oh, surely,' said the Doctor, 'with practice. You have to be very patient, you know. You really ought to have Polynesia to start you. It was she who gave me my first lessons.'

'Who is Polynesia?' I asked.

'Polynesia was a West African parrot I had. She isn't with me any more now,' said the Doctor sadly.

'Why – is she dead?'

'Oh, no,' said the Doctor. 'She is still living, I hope. But when we reached Africa she seemed so glad to get back to her own country. She wept for joy. I left her in Africa. Ah well! I have missed her terribly. She wept again when we left. But I think I did the right thing. She was one of the best friends I ever had. It was she who first gave me the idea of learning the animal-languages and becoming an animal-doctor. Good old Polynesia! A most extraordinary bird. Well, well!'

Just at that moment we heard the noise of someone running behind us; and turning round we saw Jip the dog rushing down the road after us, as fast as his legs could bring him. He seemed very excited about something, and as soon as he came up to us, he started barking and whining to the Doctor in a peculiar way.

Then the Doctor too seemed to get all worked up and began talking and making queer signs to the dog. At length he turned to me, his face shining with happiness.

'Polynesia has come back!' he cried. 'Imagine it. Jip says she has just arrived at the house. My! And it's five years since I saw her. Excuse me a minute.'

He turned as if to go back home. But the parrot, Polynesia, was already flying towards us. The Doctor clapped his hands like a child getting a new toy; while the swarm of sparrows in the roadway fluttered, gossiping, up on to the fences, highly scandalized to see a grey-and-scarlet parrot skimming down an English lane.

On she came, straight on to the Doctor's shoulder, where she immediately began talking a steady stream in a language I could not understand. She seemed to have a terrible lot to say. And very soon the Doctor had forgotten all about me and my squirrel and Jip and everything else; till at length the bird clearly asked him something about me.

'Oh, excuse me, Stubbins!' said the Doctor. 'I was so interested listening to my old friend here. We must get on and see this squirrel of yours – Polynesia, this is Thomas Stubbins.'

The parrot, on the Doctor's shoulder, nodded gravely towards me and then, to my great surprise, said quite plainly in English:

'How do you do? I remember the night you were born. It was a terribly cold winter. You were a very ugly baby.'

'Stubbins is anxious to learn animal-language,' said the Doctor. 'I was just telling him about you and the lessons you gave me when Jip ran up and told us you had arrived.'

'Well,' said the parrot, turning to me, 'I may have started the Doctor learning but I never could have done even that, if he hadn't first taught me to understand what *I* was saying when I spoke English. You see, many parrots can talk like a person, but very few of them understand what they are saying. They just say it because – well, because they fancy it is smart or because they know they will get crackers given them.'

By this time we had turned and were going towards my home with Jip running in front and Polynesia still perched on the

Doctor's shoulder. The bird chattered incessantly, mostly about Africa; but now she spoke in English, out of politeness to me.

'And how is Chee-Chee getting on? – Chee-Chee,' added the Doctor in explanation to me, "was a pet monkey I had years ago. I left him in Africa when I came away.'

'Well,' said Polynesia frowning, 'Chee-Chee is not entirely happy. I saw a good deal of him the last few years. He got dreadfully homesick for you and the house and the garden. It's funny, but I was just the same way myself. You remember how crazy I was to get back to the dear old land? And Africa *is* a wonderful country – I don't care what anybody says. Well, I thought I was going to have a perfectly grand time. But somehow – I don't know – after a few weeks it seemed to get tiresome. I just couldn't seem to settle down. Well, to make a long story short, one night I made up my mind that I'd come back here and find you. So I hunted up old Chee-Chee and told him about it. He said he didn't blame me a bit – felt exactly the same way himself.

'When I left, poor old Chee-Chee broke down and cried. He said he felt as though his only friend were leaving him – though, as you know, he has simply millions of relatives there. He said it didn't seem fair that I should have wings to fly over here any time I liked, and him with no way to follow me. But mark my words, I wouldn't be a bit surprised if he found a way to come – some day. He's a smart lad, is Chee-Chee.'

At this point we arrived at my home. My father's shop was closed and the shutters were up; but my mother was standing at the door looking down the street.

'Good evening, Mrs Stubbins,' said the Doctor. 'It is my fault your son is so late. I made him stay to supper while his clothes were drying. He was soaked to the skin; and so was I. We ran into one another in the storm and I insisted on his coming into my house for shelter.'

'I was beginning to get worried about him,' said my mother. 'I am thankful to you, sir, for looking after him so well and bringing him home.'

'Don't mention it – don't mention it,' said the Doctor. 'We have had a very interesting chat.'

'Who might it be that I have the honour of addressing?' asked my mother, staring at the grey parrot perched on the Doctor's shoulder.

'Oh, I'm John Dolittle. I dare say your husband will remember me. He made me some very excellent boots about four years ago. They really are splendid,' added the Doctor, gazing down at his feet with great satisfaction.

'The Doctor has come to cure my squirrel, Mother,' said I. 'He knows all about animals.'

'Oh, no,' said the Doctor, 'not all, Stubbins, not all about them by any means.'

'It is very kind of you to come so far to look after his pet,' said my mother. 'Tom is always bringing home strange creatures from the woods and the field.'

'Is he?' said the Doctor. 'Perhaps he will grow up to be a naturalist some day. Who knows?'

Then I led the Doctor to my bedroom at the top of the house and showed him the squirrel in the packing-case filled with straw.

The animal, who had always seemed very much afraid of me – though I had tried hard to make him feel at home – sat up at once when the Doctor came into the room and started to chatter. The Doctor chattered back in the same way and the squirrel, when he was lifted up to have his leg examined, appeared to be rather pleased than frightened.

I held a candle while the Doctor tied the leg up in what he called 'splints', which he made out of match-sticks with his penknife.

'I think you will find that his leg will get better now in a very short time,' said the Doctor closing up his bag. 'Don't let him run about for at least two weeks yet, but keep him in the open air and cover him up with dry leaves if the nights get cool. He tells me he is rather lonely here, all by himself, and is wondering how his wife and children are getting on. I have assured him you are a man to be trusted; and I will send a squirrel who lives

He sat up and started to chatter

in my garden to find out how his family are and to bring him news of them. He must be kept cheerful at all costs. Squirrels are naturally a very cheerful, active race. It is very hard for them to lie still doing nothing. But you needn't worry about him. He will be all right.'

After we had seen the Doctor out at the front door, we all came back into the parlour and talked about him till midnight.

ARE YOU A GOOD NOTICER?

THE next morning, although I had gone to bed so late the night before, I was up frightfully early. The first sparrows were just beginning to chirp sleepily on the slates outside my attic window when I jumped out of bed and scrambled into my clothes.

I could hardly wait to get back to the little house with the big garden – to see the Doctor and his animal family. For the first time in my life I forgot all about breakfast; and creeping down the stairs on tiptoe, so as not to wake my mother and father, I opened the front door and popped out into the empty, silent street.

When I got to the Doctor's house I looked into the garden. No one seemed to be about. So I opened the gate quietly and went inside.

As I turned to the left to go down a path between some hedges, I heard a voice quite close to me say,

'Good morning. How early you are!'

I turned around, and there, sitting on the top of a privet hedge, was the grey parrot, Polynesia.

'Good morning,' I said. 'I suppose I am rather early. Is the Doctor still in bed?'

'Oh, no,' said Polynesia. 'He has been up an hour and a half. You'll find him in the house somewhere. The front door is open. Just push it and go in. He is sure to be in the kitchen cooking breakfast – or working in his study. Walk right in.'

'Thank you,' I said. 'I'll go and look for him.'

When I opened the front door I could smell bacon frying. So I made my way to the kitchen. The Doctor was pouring the hot water from a kettle into the teapot.

'Good morning, Stubbins,' said he. 'Have you had your breakfast yet?'

I told the Doctor that I had forgotten all about it, so he passed the rack of toast towards me and said: 'Sit down and join me. Have some bacon.'

That was the second time I had seen the Doctor and it was the second time we had eaten together. From then on, and for many years to come, I was to sit at the Doctor's table in Puddleby – and in many strange places all over the world.

Just at that moment Polynesia came into the room and said something to the Doctor in bird-language. Of course I did not understand what it was. But the Doctor at once put down his knife and fork and left the room.

'You know, it is an awful shame,' said the parrot as soon as the Doctor had closed the door. 'Directly he comes back home, all the animals over the whole countryside get to hear of it and every sick cat and mangy rabbit for miles around comes to see him and ask his advice. Now there's a big fat hare outside at the back door with a squawking baby. Can she see the Doctor, please! Thinks it's going to have convulsions. Stupid little thing's been eating Deadly Nightshade again, I suppose. The animals are so inconsiderate at times – especially the mothers. They come round and call the Doctor away from his meals and wake him out of his bed at all hours of the night. I don't know how he stands it – really I don't. Put the Doctor's bacon down by the fire, will you? – to keep hot till he comes back.'

'Do you think I would ever be able to learn the language of the animals?' I asked, laying the plate upon the hearth.

'Well, it all depends,' said Polynesia. 'Are you clever at lessons?'

'I don't know,' I answered, feeling rather ashamed. 'You see, I've never been to school. My father is too poor to send me.'

'Well,' said the parrot, 'I don't suppose you have really missed much – to judge from what I have seen of schoolboys. But listen: are you a good noticer? Do you notice things well? I mean, for instance, supposing you saw two cock-starlings on an apple tree, and you only took one good look at them – would you be able to tell one from the other if you saw them again the next day?'

'I don't know,' I said. 'I've never tried.'

'Well that,' said Polynesia, brushing some crumbs off the corner of the table with her left foot, 'that is what you call powers of observation – noticing the small things about birds and animals; the way they walk and move their heads and flip their wings; the way they sniff the air and twitch their whiskers and wiggle their tails. You have to notice all those little things if you want to learn animal-language. That is the first thing to remember: being a good noticer is terribly important in learning animal-language.'

'It sounds pretty hard,' I said.

'You'll have to be very patient,' said Polynesia. 'It takes a long time to say even a few words properly. But if you come here often I'll give you a few lessons myself. And once you get started you'll be surprised how fast you get on. It would indeed be a good thing if you could learn. Because then you could do some of the work for the Doctor – I mean the easier work, like bandaging and giving pills. Yes, yes, that's a good idea of mine. 'T would be a great thing if the poor man could get some help – and some rest. It is a scandal the way he works. I see no reason why you shouldn't be able to help him a great deal. That is, if you are really interested in animals.'

'Oh, I'd love that!' I cried. 'Do you think the Doctor would let me?'

'Certainly,' said Polynesia, 'as soon as you have learned something about doctoring. I'll speak of it to him myself – Sh! I hear him coming. Quick – bring his bacon back on to the table.'

MY EDUCATION BEGINS

MANY weeks later and with the help of Polynesia, I began to learn the animals' languages. Oh, I was slow at first and Polynesia often scolded me for not remembering something that she had told me over and over. But gradually I could interpret all the wigglings of tails and twitching of noses and squeaks and squawks that formed the animals' messages to humans.

When I thought I was ready I asked Polynesia to speak to the Doctor on my behalf.

'Being a good noticer is terribly important'

'You mean you want to be a proper assistant to the Doctor, is that it?' she asked.

'Yes, I suppose that's what you call it,' I answered. 'You know you said yourself that you thought I could be very useful to him.'

'Humph – let's go and speak to the Doctor about it,' said Polynesia. 'He's in the next room – in the study. Open the door very gently – he may be working and not want to be disturbed.'

Presently the Doctor looked up and saw us at the door.

'Oh – come in, Stubbins,' said he. 'Did you wish to speak to me? Come in and take a chair.'

'Doctor,' I said, 'I want to be a naturalist – like you – when I grow up.'

'Oh, you do, do you?' murmured the Doctor. 'Humph – well! – Dear me! – You don't say! – Well, well! Have you, er – have you spoken to your mother and father about it?'

'No, not yet,' I said. 'I want you to speak to them for me. You would do it better. I want to be your helper – your assistant, if you'll have me.'

'What arrangement was it that you thought of?' asked the Doctor.

'Well, I thought,' said I, 'that perhaps you would come and see my mother and father and tell them that if they let me live here with you and work hard, you will teach me to read and write. You see my mother is awfully anxious to have me learn reading and writing. And besides, I couldn't be a proper naturalist without, could I?'

'Oh, I don't know so much about that,' said the Doctor. 'It is nice, I admit, to be able to read and write. But naturalists are not all alike, you know. For example: this young fellow Charles Darwin that people are talking about so much now – he's a Cambridge graduate – reads and writes very well. And then Cuvier – he used to be a tutor. But listen, the greatest naturalist of them all doesn't even know how to write his own name nor to read the A.B.C.'

'Who is he?' I asked.

'He is a mysterious person,' said the Doctor, 'a very mysterious person. His name is Long Arrow, the son of Golden Arrow. He is a Red Indian.'

'Have you ever seen him?' I asked.

'No,' said the Doctor, 'I've never seen him. No white man has ever met him. I fancy Mr Darwin doesn't even know that he exists. He lives almost entirely with the animals and with the different tribes of Indians – usually somewhere among the mountains of Peru. Never stays long in one place. Goes from tribe to tribe, like a sort of Indian tramp.'

'How do you know so much about him,' I asked, 'if you've never even seen him?'

'The Purple Bird-of-Paradise,' said the Doctor, 'she told me all about him. She says he is a perfectly marvellous naturalist. I got her to take a message to him for me last time she was here. I am expecting her back any day now. I can hardly wait to see what answer she has brought from him. It is already almost the last week of August. I do hope nothing has happened to her on the way.'

'But why do the animals and birds come to you when they are sick?' I said. 'Why don't they go to him, if he is so very wonderful?'

'It seems that my methods are more up to date,' said the Doctor. 'But from what the Purple Bird-of-Paradise tells me, Long Arrow's knowledge of natural history must be positively tremendous. His speciality is botany – plants and all that sort of thing. But he knows a lot about birds and animals too. He's very good on bees and beetles. – But now tell me, Stubbins, are you quite sure that you really want to be a naturalist?'

'Yes,' said I, 'my mind is made up.'

'Well you know, it isn't a very good profession for making money. Not at all, it isn't. Most of the good naturalists don't make any money whatever. All they do is spend money buying butterfly-nets and cases for birds' eggs and things. It is only now, after I have been a naturalist for many years, that I am beginning to make a little money from the books I write.'

'I don't care about money,' I said. 'I want to be a naturalist.' I hesitated a minute before I went on, 'You see, there's another

Swearing at the blackbird down below

thing: if I'm living with you, and sort of belong to your house and business, I shall be able to come with you next time you go on a voyage.'

'Oh, I see,' said he, smiling. 'So you want to come on a voyage with me, do you? – Ah hah!'

'I want to go on all your voyages with you. It would be much easier for you if you had someone to carry the butterfly-nets and notebooks. Wouldn't it now?'

For a long time the Doctor sat thinking, drumming on the desk with his fingers, while I waited, terribly impatiently, to see what he was going to say.

At last he shrugged his shoulders and stood up.

'Well, Stubbins,' said he, 'I'll come and talk it over with you and your parents – say – next Thursday. And – well, we'll see. We'll see.'

Then I tore home like the wind to tell my mother and father that the Doctor was coming to see them next Thursday.

The next day I was sitting on the wall of the Doctor's garden after tea, talking to Dab-Dab. Over in one corner of the garden a small sparrow was standing on the sundial swearing at some blackbird down below.

'Who is that?' I asked Dab-Dab.

'Oh, that is Cheapside!' she replied, ruffling her feathers. 'He's a cheeky, rude, London sparrow who lives around St Paul's Cathedral. But the Doctor likes him – ' She shrugged her wings. 'We put up with him because of that!'

Suddenly I heard a curious distant noise down the road, towards the town. It sounded like a lot of people cheering. I stood up on the wall to see if I could make out what was coming. Presently there appeared round a bend a great crowd of school-children following a very ragged, curious-looking woman.

'What in the world can it be?' cried Dab-Dab.

The children were all laughing and shouting. And certainly the woman they were following was most extraordinary. She had very long arms and the most stooping shoulders I have ever seen. She wore a straw hat on the side of her head with poppies on it; and her skirt was so long for her it dragged on the ground like a ball-gown's train. I could not see anything of her face because of the wide hat pulled over her eyes. But as she got nearer to us and the laughing of the children grew louder, I noticed that her hands were very dark in colour, and hairy, like a witch's.

Then all of a sudden Dab-Dab at my side startled me by crying out in a loud voice:

'Why it's Chee-Chee! – Chee-Chee come back at last! How dare those children tease him! I'll give the little imps something to laugh at!'

A traveller arrives

And she flew right off the wall down into the road and made straight for the children, squawking away in a most terrifying fashion and pecking at their feet and legs. The children made off down the street back to the town as hard as they could run.

The strange-looking figure in the straw hat stood gazing after them a moment and then came wearily up to the gate. It didn't bother to undo the latch but just climbed right over the gate as though it were something in the way. And then I noticed that it took hold of the bars with its feet, so that it really had four hands to climb with. But it was only when I at last got a glimpse of the face under the hat that I could be really sure it was a monkey.

Chee-Chee – for it was he – frowned at me suspiciously from the top of the gate, as though he thought I was going to laugh at him like the other boys and girls. Then he dropped into the garden on the inside and immediately started taking off his clothes. He tore the straw hat in two and threw it down into the road. Then he took off his bodice and skirt, and jumped on them savagely and began kicking them round the front garden.

Presently I heard a screech from the house, and out flew Polynesia, followed by the Doctor and Jip.

'Chee-Chee! – Chee-Chee!' shouted the parrot. 'You've come at last! I always told the Doctor you'd find a way. How ever did you do it?'

They all gathered round him shaking him by his four hands, laughing and asking him a million questions at once. Then they all started back for the house.

'Run up to my bedroom, Stubbins,' said the Doctor, turning to me. 'You'll find a bag of peanuts in the small left-hand drawer of the bureau. I have always kept them there in case he might come back unexpectedly some day. And wait a minute – see if Dab-Dab has any bananas in the pantry. Chee-Chee hasn't had a banana, he tells me, in two months.'

When I came down again to the kitchen I found everybody listening attentively to the monkey who was telling the story of his journey from Africa.

I BECOME A DOCTOR'S ASSISTANT

When Thursday evening came there was great excitement at our house. My mother had asked me what were the Doctor's favourite dishes, and I had told her: spare ribs, sliced beetroot, fried bread, shrimps, and treacle-tart. Tonight she had them all on the table waiting for him; and she was now fussing round the house to see if everything was tidy and in readiness for his coming.

At last we heard a knock upon the door, and of course it was I who got there first to let him in.

After supper was over (which he enjoyed very much) the table was cleared away and the washing-up left in the kitchen sink till the next day. Then the Doctor and my mother and father began talking about my future.

'Your son tells me that he is anxious to become a naturalist,' said the Doctor.

And then began a long talk which lasted far into the night. At first both my father and mother were rather against the idea – as they had been from the beginning. They said it was only a boyish whim, and that I would get tired of it very soon. But after the matter had been talked over from every side, the Doctor turned to my father and said:

'Well now, supposing, Mr Stubbins, that your son came to me for two years – that is, until he is twelve years old. During those two years he will have time to see if he is going to grow tired of it or not. Also, during that time, I will promise to teach him reading and writing and perhaps a little arithmetic as well.'

Then my mother spoke up. She pointed out to my father that this was a grand chance for me to get learning.

'Tommy can easily spare these two years for his education; and if he learns no more than to read and write, the time will not be lost.'

Well, at length my father gave in; and it was agreed that I was to go to live at the Doctor's house for the two years.

Of course it was I who got there first to let him in

There surely was never a happier boy in the world than I was at that moment. At last the dream of my life was to come true! At last I was to be given a chance to seek my fortune, to have adventure! For I knew perfectly well that it was now almost time for the Doctor to start upon another voyage. Polynesia had told me that he hardly ever stayed home for more than six months at a stretch. Therefore he would surely be going again within a fortnight. And I – I, Tommy Stubbins, would go with him. Just to think of it! – to cross the sea, to walk on foreign shores, to roam the world!

The next day I moved to the Doctor's house and from then on – for many years after – my time was filled with study and happy companionship with all the animals of the household as I learned more and more to speak their language.

The Doctor's friends became my friends and I never found time again to waste as I had done during the past ten years of my life.

Among these friends was Luke the Hermit. He was a peculiar person. Far out on the marshes he lived in a little bit of a shack – all alone except for his brindle bulldog. He never came into town; never seemed to want to talk to people. His dog, Bob, drove them away if they came near his hut.

Nevertheless there were two people who often went out to that little shack on the fens: the Doctor and myself. And Bob the bulldog never barked when he heard us coming. For we liked Luke; and Luke liked us.

One day, when the Doctor, Jip and I went to Luke's shack to pay him a visit, we found him and Bob, his dog, gone. The shack door was open and swinging dismally in the wind.

This didn't surprise the Doctor too much, until he noticed that Jip was acting queerly.

'What's wrong, Jip?' the Doctor asked.

'Nothing much – nothing worth speaking of,' said Jip, examining the hut extremely carefully.

Well, we left the marsh and on our way home missed Jip.

'That's peculiar,' said the Doctor. 'He must know something we don't.'

Just as we were sitting down to luncheon in the kitchen we heard a great racket at the front door. I ran and opened it. In bounded Jip.

'Doctor!' cried Jip (he was badly out of breath from running). 'I know all about the Hermit – I have known for years. But I couldn't tell you.'

'Why?' asked the Doctor.

'Because I'd promised not to tell anyone. It was Bob, his dog, that told me. And I swore to him that I would keep the secret.'

We found the door open, swinging in the wind

'Well, and are you going to tell me now?'

'Yes,' said Jip, 'we've got to save him. I followed Bob's scent just now when I left you out there on the marshes. And I found him. And I said to him, "Is it all right," I said, "for me to tell the Doctor now? Maybe he can do something." And Bob says to me, "Yes," said he, "it's all right because – " '

'Oh, for heaven's sake, go on, go on!' cried the Doctor. 'Tell us what the mystery is – not what you said to Bob and what Bob said to you. What has happened? Where is the Hermit?'

'He's in Puddleby Jail,' said Jip. 'He's in prison.'

'In prison!'

'Yes.'

'What for? What's he done?'

Jip went over to the door and smelt at the bottom of it to see if anyone were listening outside. Then he came back to the Doctor on tiptoe and whispered,

'He killed a man!'

'Lord preserve us!' cried the Doctor, sitting down heavily in a chair and mopping his forehead with a handkerchief. 'When did he do it?'

'Fifteen years ago – in a Mexican gold-mine. That's why he has been a hermit ever since. He shaved off his beard and kept away from people out there on the marshes so he wouldn't be recognized. But last week, it seems these new-fangled policemen came to Town; and they heard there was a strange man who kept to himself all alone in a shack on the fen. And they got suspicious. For a long time people had been hunting all over the world for the man that did that killing in the Mexican gold-mine fifteen years ago. So these policemen went out to the shack, and they recognized Luke by a mole on his arm. And they took him to prison.'

'Well, well!' murmured the Doctor. 'Who would have thought it? – Luke, the philosopher! – Killed a man! – I can hardly believe it.'

'It's true enough – unfortunately,' said Jip. 'Luke did it. But it wasn't his fault. Bob says so. And he was there and saw it all. He was scarcely more than a puppy at the time. Bob says Luke couldn't help it. He *had* to do it.'

'Where is Bob now?' asked the Doctor.

'Down at the prison. I wanted him to come with me here to see you; but he won't leave the prison while Luke is there. Bob says he thinks they are going to kill Luke for a punishment if they can prove that he did it – or certainly keep him in prison for the rest of his life. Won't you please come? Perhaps if you spoke to the judge and told him what a good man Luke really is they'd let him off.'

'Of course I'll come,' said the Doctor getting up and moving to go. 'But I'm very much afraid that I shan't be of any real help.' He turned at the door and hesitated thoughtfully.

'And yet – I wonder –'

Then he opened the door and passed out with Jip and me close at his heels.

MENDOZA

AFTER working our way through the great crowd gathered around the Court-house we got to see Luke.

Outside the door of Luke's cell we found Bob, the bulldog, who wagged his tail sadly when he saw us. In the cell on the bed sat the Hermit.

Then the Doctor talked to Luke for more than half an hour, trying to cheer him up; while I sat around wondering what I ought to say and wishing I could do something.

At last the Doctor said he wanted to see Bob; and we knocked upon the door and were let out by the policeman.

'Bob,' said the Doctor to the big bulldog in the passage, 'come out with me into the porch. I want to ask you something.'

'How is he, Doctor?' asked Bob as we walked down the corridor into the Court-house porch.

'Oh, Luke's all right. Very miserable of course, but he's all right. Now tell me, Bob, you saw this business happen, didn't you? You were there when the man was killed, eh?'

'I was, Doctor,' said Bob, 'and I tell you –'

'All right,' the Doctor interrupted, 'that's all I want to know for the present. There isn't time to tell me more now. The trial is just going to begin. There are the judge and the lawyers coming up the steps. Now listen, Bob: I want you to stay with me when I go into the court-room. And whatever I tell you to do, do it. Do you understand? Don't bite anybody, no matter what they may say about Luke. Just behave perfectly quietly and answer any questions I may ask you – truthfully. Do you understand?'

'Very well. But do you think you will be able to get him off,

Doctor? 'asked Bob. 'He's a good man, Doctor. He really is. There never was a better.'

'We'll see, we'll see, Bob. It's a new thing I'm going to try. I'm not sure the judge will allow it. But – well, we'll see. It's time to go into the court-room now. Don't forget what I told you. Remember: for heaven's sake don't start biting anyone or you'll get us all put out and spoil everything.'

Inside the court-room everything was very solemn and wonderful. It was a high, big room. Raised above the floor, against the wall, was the judge's desk; and there the judge was already sitting – an old handsome man in a marvellous big wig of grey hair and a gown of black. Below him was another wide, long desk at which lawyers in white wigs sat. The whole thing reminded me of a mixture between a church and a school.

'Those twelve men at the side,' whispered the Doctor, "those in pews like a choir, they are what is called the jury. It is they who decide whether Luke is guilty – whether he did it or not.'

'And look!' I said. 'There's Luke himself in a sort of pulpit-thing with policemen each side of him. And there's another pulpit, the same kind, the other side of the room, see – only that one's empty.'

'That one is called the witness-box,' said the Doctor. 'Now I'm going down to speak to one of those men in white wigs; and I want you to wait here and keep these two seats for us. Bob will stay with you. Keep an eye on him – better hold on to his collar. I shan't be more than a minute or so.'

With that the Doctor disappeared into the crowd which filled the main part of the room.

Then I saw the judge take up a funny little wooden hammer and knock on his desk with it. This, it seemed, was to make people keep quiet, for immediately everyone stopped buzzing and talking and began to listen very respectfully. Then another man in a black gown stood up and began reading from a paper in his hand.

He mumbled away exactly as though he were saying his prayers and didn't want any one to understand what language they were in. But I managed to catch a few words:

'Biz – biz – biz – biz – biz – otherwise known as Luke the Hermit, of biz – biz – biz – biz – for killing his partner with biz – biz – biz – otherwise known as Bluebeard Bill on the night of the biz – biz – biz – in the biz – biz – biz – of Mexico. Therefore His Majesty's – biz – biz – biz – '

At this moment I felt someone take hold of my arm from the back, and turning round I found the Doctor had returned with one of the men in white wigs.

'Stubbins, this is Mr Percy Jenkyns,' said the Doctor. 'He is Luke's lawyer. It is his business to get Luke off – if he can.'

Mr Jenkyns seemed to be an extremely young man with a round smooth face like a boy. He shook hands with me and then immediately turned and went on talking with the Doctor.

'Oh, I think it is a perfectly precious idea,' he was saying. 'Of *course* the dog must be admitted as a witness; he was the only one who saw the thing take place. I'm awfully glad you came. I wouldn't have missed this for anything. My hat! Won't it make the old court sit up? They're always frightfully dull, these Assizes. But this will stir things. A bulldog witness for the defence! I do hope there are plenty of reporters present – yes, there's one making a sketch of the prisoner. I shall become known after this. And won't Conkey be pleased? My hat!'

He put his hand over his mouth to smother a laugh and his eyes fairly sparkled with mischief.

'Who is Conkey?' I asked the Doctor.

'Sh! He is speaking of the judge up there, the Honourable Eustace Beauchamp Conckley.'

The proceedings for the next step were routine: the prosecutor trying his best to get Luke into trouble and Luke's lawyer, Mr Jenkyns, popping up and down, crying, 'Objection!'

Most of the time I could hardly keep my eyes off poor Luke, who sat there between his two policemen, staring at the floor as though he weren't interested. The only time I saw him take any notice at all was when a small dark man with wicked little watery eyes got up into the witness-box. I heard Bob snarl under my chair as this person came into the court-room and Luke's eyes just blazed with anger and contempt.

A small man with wicked little watery eyes

This man said his name was Mendoza and that he was the one who had guided the Mexican police to the mine after Bluebeard Bill had been killed. And at every word he said I could hear Bob down below me muttering between his teeth,

'It's a lie! It's a lie! I'll chew his face. It's a lie!'

And both the Doctor and I had hard work keeping the dog under the seat.

Then I noticed that our Mr Jenkyns had disappeared from the Doctor's side. But presently I saw him stand up at the long table to speak to the judge.

'Your Honour,' said he, 'I wish to introduce a new witness for the defence, Doctor John Dolittle, the naturalist. Will you please step into the witness-box, Doctor?'

There was a buzz of excitement as the Doctor made his way across the crowded room; and I noticed the nasty lawyer with the long nose lean down and whisper something to a friend, smiling in an ugly way which made me want to pinch him.

Then Mr Jenkyns asked the Doctor a whole lot of questions about himself and made him answer in a loud voice so the whole court could hear. He finished up by saying:

'And you are prepared to swear, Doctor Dolittle, that you understand the language of dogs and can make them understand you. Is that so?'

'Yes,' said the Doctor, 'that is so.'

'And what, might I ask,' put in the judge in a very quiet, dignified voice, 'has all this to do with the killing of, er – er – Bluebeard Bill?'

'This, your Honour,' said Mr Jenkyns, talking in a very grand manner as though he were on a stage in a theatre: 'there is in this court-room at the present moment a bulldog who was the only living thing that saw the man killed. With the Court's permission I propose to put that dog in the witness-stand and have him questioned before you by the eminent scientist, Doctor John Dolittle.'

THE JUDGE'S DOG

At first there was a dead silence in the Court. Then everybody began whispering or giggling at the same time, till the whole room sounded like a great hive of bees. Many people seemed to be shocked; most of them were amused; and a few were angry.

Presently up sprang the nasty lawyer with the long nose.

'I protest, Your Honour,' he cried, waving his arms wildly to the judge. 'I object. The dignity of this court is in peril. I protest.'

'I am the one to take care of the dignity of this court,' said the judge.

Then Mr Jenkyns got up again. (If it hadn't been such a serious matter, it was almost like a Punch-and-Judy show – somebody was always popping down and somebody else popping up.)

'If there is any doubt on the score of our being able to do as we say, Your Honour will have no objection, I trust, to the Doctor's giving the Court a demonstration of his powers – of showing that he actually can understand the speech of animals?'

I thought I saw a twinkle of amusement come into the old judge's eyes as he sat considering a moment before he answered.

'No,' he said at last, 'I don't think so.' Then he turned to the Doctor.

'Are you quite sure you can do this?' he asked.

'Quite, Your Honour,' said the Doctor, 'quite sure.'

'Very well then,' said the judge. 'If you can satisfy us that you really are able to understand canine testimony, the dog shall be admitted as a witness.'

'I protest, I protest!' yelled the long-nosed prosecutor. 'This is a scandal, an outrage to the Bar!'

'Sit down!' said the judge in a very stern voice.

'What animal does Your Honour wish me to talk with?' asked the Doctor.

'I would like you to talk to my own dog,' said the judge. 'He is outside in the cloak-room. I will have him brought in; and then we shall see what you can do.'

Then someone went out and fetched the judge's dog, a lovely great Russian wolf-hound with slender legs and a shaggy coat. He was a proud and beautiful creature.

'Now, Doctor,' said the judge, 'did you ever see this dog before? – Remember you are in the witness-stand and under oath.'

'No, Your Honour, I never saw him before.'

'Very well then, will you please ask him to tell you what I had for supper last night? He was with me and watched me while I ate.'

He was a proud and beautiful creature

Then the Doctor and the dog started talking to one another in signs and sounds; and they kept at it for quite a long time. And the Doctor began to giggle and get so interested that he seemed to forget all about the Court and the judge and everything else.

'Haven't you finished yet?' the judge asked the Doctor. 'It shouldn't take that long just to ask what I had for supper.'

'Oh, no, Your Honour,' said the Doctor. 'The dog told me that long ago. But then he went on to tell me what you did after supper.'

'Never mind that,' said the judge. 'Tell me what answer he gave you to my question.'

'He says you had a mutton-chop, two baked potatoes, a pickled walnut and a glass of ale.'

The Honourable Eustace Beauchamp Conckley went white to the lips.

'Sounds like witchcraft,' he muttered. 'I never dreamed – '

'And after your supper,' the Doctor went on, 'he says you went to see a prize-fight and then sat up playing cards for money till twelve o'clock and came home singing, "We won't get – " '

'That will do,' the judge interrupted. 'I am satisfied you can do as you say. The prisoner's dog shall be admitted as a witness.'

'I protest, I object!' screamed the prosecutor. 'Your Honour, this is – '

'Sit down!' roared the judge. 'I say the dog shall be heard. That ends the matter. Put the witness in the stand.'

And then for the first time in the solemn history of England a dog was put in the witness-stand of His Majesty's Court of Assizes. And it was I, Tommy Stubbins (when the Doctor made a sign to me across the room) who proudly led Bob up the aisle, through the astonished crowd, past the frowning, spluttering, long-nosed prosecutor, and made him comfortable on a high chair in the witness-box, from where the old bulldog sat scowling down over the rail upon the amazed and gaping jury.

The trial went swiftly forward after that. Mr Jenkyns told the Doctor to ask Bob what he saw on the 'night of the 29th'; and when Bob had told all he knew and the Doctor had turned it into English for the judge and the jury, this was what he had to say:

'My master, Luke Fitzjohn (otherwise known as Luke the Hermit) and his two partners, Manuel Mendoza and William Boggs (otherwise known as Bluebeard Bill) had found gold in a mine they had been digging.

'I had always suspected these two men of being bad and one day I heard them plotting to kill Luke and keep all the gold for themselves.

'Because Luke couldn't understand dog-language I never let him out of my sight, day or night.

'One day when Luke was hauling up the bucket which they used to bring one another – or the gold – to the surface, I saw Mendoza come out of the hut where we all lived. Mendoza thought Bill was away buying groceries. But he wasn't: he was in the bucket. When Mendoza saw Luke hauling and straining on the rope he thought he was pulling up a bucketful of gold. So he drew a pistol from his pocket and came sneaking up behind Luke to shoot him.

'I did a thing I've never done before: suddenly and savagely I bit my master in the leg from behind. Luke was so hurt and startled that he let go the rope and, *CRASH!* down went Bill in the bucket to the bottom of the mine and he was killed.

'While my master was busy scolding me Mendoza put his pistol in his pocket, came up with a smile on his face and looked down the mine.

' "Why, good gracious!" said he to Luke. "You've killed Bluebeard Bill. I must go and tell the police" – hoping, you see, to get the whole mine to himself when Luke should be put in prison. Then he jumped on his horse and galloped away.

'So while Mendoza was gone Luke and I stole away together secretly and came to England. Here he shaved off his beard and became a hermit. And ever since, for fifteen years, we've remained in hiding. This is all I have to say. And I swear it is the truth, every word.'

In the middle of all this up got the horrible prosecutor again, waving his arms more wildly than ever.

'Your Honour,' he cried, 'I must object to this evidence as biased. Of course the dog would not tell the truth against his own master. I object. I protest.'

'Very well,' said the judge, 'you are at liberty to cross-examine It is your duty as prosecutor to prove his evidence untrue. There is the dog: question him, if you do not believe what he says.'

I thought the long-nosed lawyer would have a fit. He looked first at the dog, then at the Doctor, then at the judge, then back at the dog scowling from the witness-box. He opened his mouth to say something; but no words came. He waved his arms some more. His face got redder and redder. At last, clutching his forehead, he sank weakly into his seat and had to be helped out of the court-room by two friends. As he was half carried through the door he was still feebly murmuring, 'I protest – I object – I protest!'

Well, Luke was set free and everyone cheered: three cheers for Luke the Hermit: Hooray! – Three cheers for his dog: Hooray! – Three cheers for the Doctor: Hooray! Hooray! HOO–R–A–Y!

THE PURPLE BIRD-OF-PARADISE

POLYNESIA was waiting for us in the front porch. She looked full of important news.

'Doctor,' said she, 'the Purple Bird-of-Paradise has arrived!'

'At last!' said the Doctor. 'I had begun to fear some accident had befallen her. And how is Miranda?'

'Oh, she seemed all right when she arrived,' said Polynesia, 'but the mischief-making sparrow, Cheapside, insulted her as soon as she came into the garden. She's in the study now. And I shut Cheapside in one of your bookcases – you can deal with *him*!'

In the centre of the study table, perched on the ink-stand, stood the most beautiful bird I have ever seen. She had a deep violet-coloured breast, scarlet wings and a long, long sweeping tail of gold. Already she had her head tucked under her wing.

'Sh!' said Dab-Dab. 'Miranda is asleep.'

The noisy little sparrow was fluttering angrily against the glass of the bookcase.

'Let Cheapside out, please,' whispered the Doctor.

Dab-Dab opened the bookcase door and the sparrow strutted out trying hard not to look guilty.

'Cheapside,' said the Doctor sternly, 'what did you say to Miranda?'

'I didn't say nothin', Doc, straight I didn't. That is, nothin' much. She comes swankin' into the garden, turnin' up 'er nose in all directions. And all I said was, "You don't belong in an English garden; you ought to be in a milliner's shop." That's all!'

'You should be ashamed of yourself, Cheapside,' said the Doctor. 'Leave the room!'

Sheepishly, but still trying to look as though he didn't care, Cheapside hopped out into the passage and Dab-Dab closed the door.

The Doctor went up to the beautiful bird on the ink-stand and gently stroked its back. Instantly its head popped out from under its wing.

'Well, Miranda,' said the Doctor, 'I'm terribly sorry this has happened. But you mustn't mind Cheapside; he doesn't know any better. He's a city bird; and all his life he has had to squabble for a living. You must make allowances.'

Miranda stretched her gorgeous wings wearily. Now that I saw her awake and moving I noticed what a superior, well-bred manner she had. There were tears in her eyes and her beak was trembling.

'I wouldn't have minded so much,' she said in a high silvery voice, 'if I hadn't been so dreadfully worn out – that and something else,' she added beneath her breath.

'Did you have a hard time getting here?' asked the Doctor.

'The worst passage I ever made,' said Miranda. 'The weather – well there. What's the use? I'm here anyway.'

'Tell me,' said the Doctor as though he had been impatiently waiting to say something for a long time, "what did Long Arrow say when you gave him my message?'

The Purple Bird-of-Paradise hung her head.

'That's the worst part of it,' she said. 'I might almost as well have not come at all. I wasn't able to deliver your message. I couldn't find him. Long Arrow, the son of Golden Arrow, has disappeared!'

'Disappeared!' cried the Doctor. 'Why, what's become of him?'

'Nobody knows,' Miranda answered. 'He had often disappeared before, as I have told you – so that the Indians didn't know where he was. But it's a mighty hard thing to hide away from the birds. I had always been able to find some owl or martin who could tell me where he was – if I wanted to know. But not this time. That's why I'm nearly a fortnight late in coming to you: I kept hunting and hunting, asking everywhere. I went over the whole length and breadth of South America. But there wasn't a living thing could tell me where he was.'

There was a sad silence in the room after she had finished; the Doctor was frowning in a peculiar sort of way and Polynesia scratched her head.

'Did you ask the black parrots?' asked Polynesia. 'They usually know everything.'

'Certainly I did,' said Miranda. 'And I was so upset at not being able to find out anything, that I forgot all about observing the weather-signs before I started my flight here. I didn't even bother to break my journey at the Azores, but cut right across, making for the Straits of Gibraltar – as though it were June or July. And of course I ran into a perfectly frightful storm in mid-Atlantic. I really thought I'd never come through it. Luckily I found a piece of a wrecked vessel floating in the sea after the storm had partly died down; and I roosted on it and took some sleep. If I hadn't been able to take that rest I wouldn't be here to tell the tale.'

'Poor Miranda. What a time you must have had!' said the Doctor. 'But tell me, were you able to find out whereabouts Long Arrow was last seen?'

'Yes. A young albatross told me he had seen him on Spidermonkey Island.'

'Spidermonkey Island? That's somewhere off the coast of Brazil, isn't it?'

'Yes, that's it. Of course I flew there right away and asked every bird on the island – and it is a big island, a hundred miles long. I nearly got caught and put in a cage for my pains too. That's the worst of having beautiful feathers: it's as much as your life is worth to go near most humans. They say, 'Oh, how pretty!" and shoot an arrow or bullet into you. You and Long

'What else can I think?'

Arrow were the only men that I would ever trust myself near – out of all the people in the world.'

'But you don't really think that he is dead, do you?' asked the Doctor.

'What else can I think,' asked Miranda, bursting into tears, 'when for six whole months he has not been seen by flesh, fish or fowl?'

BLIND TRAVEL

THIS news about Long Arrow made us all very sad. And I could see from the silent dreamy way the Doctor took his tea that he was dreadfully upset.

I did my best to cheer him up by reminding him about our plans for a voyage.

'But you see, Stubbins,' said he as we rose from the table and Dab-Dab and Chee-Chee began to clear away, 'I don't know where to go now. I feel sort of lost since Miranda brought me this news. On this voyage I had planned going to see Long Arrow. I had been looking forward to it for a whole year. I felt he might help me in learning the language of the shellfish – and perhaps in finding some way of getting to the bottom of the sea. But now? – He's gone! And all his great knowledge has gone with him.'

Then he seemed to fall a-dreaming again.

We went back into the study, where Jip brought the Doctor his slippers and his pipe. And after the pipe was lit and the smoke began to fill the room the old man seemed to cheer up a little.

'But you will go on some voyage, Doctor, won't you,' I asked, 'even if you can't go to find Long Arrow?'

He looked up sharply into my face; and I suppose he saw how anxious I was. Because he suddenly smiled his old boyish smile and said,

'Yes, Stubbins. Don't worry. We'll go. We mustn't stop working and learning, even if poor Long Arrow has disappeared. But where to go: that's the question. Where shall we go?'

There were so many places that I wanted to go that I couldn't make up my mind right away. And while I was still thinking, the Doctor said, 'I'll tell you what we'll do, Stubbins: it's a game I used to play when I was young – before Sarah came to live with me. I used to call it Blind Travel. Whenever I wanted to go on a voyage, and couldn't make up my mind where to go, I would take the atlas and open it with my eyes shut. Next, I'd wave a pencil, still without looking, and stick it down on whatever page had fallen open. Then I'd open my eyes and look. It's a very exciting game, is Blind Travel. Because you have to swear, before you begin, that you will go to the place the pencil touches, come what may. Shall we play it?'

'Oh, let's!' I almost yelled. 'How thrilling! I hope it's China – or Borneo – or Baghdad.'

And in a moment I had scrambled up the bookcase, dragged the big atlas from the top shelf and laid it on the table before the Doctor.

I knew every page in that atlas by heart. How many days and nights I had lingered over its old faded maps, following the blue rivers from the mountains to the sea: wondering what the little towns really looked like, and how wide were the sprawling lakes! I had had a lot of fun with that atlas, travelling, in my mind, all over the world.

As the Doctor began sharpening his pencil a thought came to me.

'What if the pencil falls upon the North Pole?' I asked. 'Will we have to go there?'

'No. The rules of the game say you don't have to go any place you've been before. You are allowed another try. I've been to the North Pole,' he ended quietly, 'so we shan't have to go there.'

I could hardly speak with astonishment.

'*You've been to the North Pole!*' I managed to gasp out at last. 'But I thought it was still undiscovered. The map shows all the places explorers have reached to, *trying* to get there. Why isn't your name down if you discovered it?'

In a moment I had scrambled up the bookcase

'I promised to keep it a secret. And you must promise me never to tell anyone. Yes, I discovered the North Pole in April 1809. But shortly after I got there the polar bears came to me in a body and told me there was a great deal of coal there, buried beneath the snow. They knew, they said, that human beings would do anything, and go anywhere, to get coal. So would I please keep it a secret. Because once people began coming up there to start coal-mines, their beautiful white country would be spoiled – and there was nowhere else in the world cold enough for polar bears to be comfortable. So of course I had to promise them I would. Well now, are we ready? – Good! Take the pencil and stand here close to the table. When the book falls open, wave the pencil round three times and jab it down. Ready? – All right. Shut your eyes.'

It was a tense and fearful moment – but very thrilling. We both had our eyes shut tight. I heard the atlas fall open with a bang. I wondered what page it was: England or Asia. If it should be the map of Asia, so much would depend on where that pencil would land. I waved three times in a circle. I began to lower my hand. The pencil-point touched the page.

'All right,' I called out, 'it's done.'

We both opened our eyes; then bumped our heads together with a crack in our eagerness to lean over and see where we were to go.

The atlas lay open at a map called, *Chart of the South Atlantic Ocean.* My pencil-point was resting right in the centre of a tiny island. The name of it was printed so small that the Doctor had to get out his strong spectacles to read it. I was trembling with excitement.

'*Spidermonkey Island,*' he read out slowly. Then he whistled softly beneath his breath. 'Of all the extraordinary things. You've hit upon the very island where Long Arrow was last seen on earth – I wonder – Well, well! How very singular! – Well, there's one good thing about it: I shall be able to get some Jabizri beetles.'

'What are Jabizri beetles?'

'They are a very rare kind of beetle with peculiar habits. I want to study them. There are only three countries in the world where they are to be found. Spidermonkey Island is one of them. But even there they are very scarce.'

'What is this little question-mark after the name of the island for?' I asked, pointing to the map.

'That means that the island's position in the ocean is not known very exactly – that it is somewhere *about* there.'

At this point the poor Bird-of-Paradise stirred and woke up. In our excitement we had forgotten to speak low.

At the door I tripped over Dab-Dab

'We are going to Spidermonkey Island, Miranda,' said the Doctor. 'You know where it is, do you not?'

'I know where it was the last time I saw it,' said the bird. 'But whether it will be there still, I can't say.'

'What do you mean?' asked the Doctor. 'It is always in the same place surely?'

'Not by any means,' said Miranda. 'Why, didn't you know? – Spidermonkey Island is a *floating* island. It moves all over the place – usually somewhere near southern South America. But of course I could surely find it for you if you want to go there.'

At this fresh piece of news I could contain myself no longer. I was bursting to tell someone. I ran dancing and singing from the room to find Chee-Chee.

At the door I tripped over Dab-Dab, who was just coming in with her wings full of plates, and fell headlong on my nose.

'Has the boy gone crazy?' cried the duck. 'Where do you think you're going, ninny?'

'To Spidermonkey Island!' I shouted, picking myself up and doing cart-wheels down the hall. 'Spidermonkey Island! Hooray! – And it's a *floating* island!'

'You're going to Bedlam, I should say,' snorted the housekeeper. 'Look what you've done to my best china!'

But I was far too happy to listen to her scolding; and I ran on, singing, into the kitchen to find Chee-Chee.

THE 'CURLEW'

THAT same week we began our preparations for the voyage.

'Suppose we go down and see your friend Joe, the mussel-man,' said the Doctor. 'He will know about boats.'

'I'd like to come too,' said Jip.

'All right, come along,' said the Doctor and off we went.

Joe said he had a boat – one he had just bought – but it needed three people to sail her. We told him we wanted to see it anyway.

So the mussel-man took us off a little way down the river and showed us the neatest, prettiest little vessel that ever was built. She was called the *Curlew*. Joe said he would sell her to us cheap. But the trouble was that the boat needed three people, while we were only two.

'Of course I shall be taking Chee-Chee,' said the Doctor. 'But although he is very quick and clever, he is not as strong as a man. We really ought to have another person to sail a boat as big as that.'

'There's Matthew Mugg, the Cat's-meat-Man,' I said.

'No, he wouldn't do. Matthew's a very wise fellow, but he

talks too much – mostly about his rheumatism. You have to be frightfully particular whom you take with you on long voyages.'

Well, in the end, the Doctor bought the *Curlew* and we began at once to provision her. And for three whole days we carried sacks of flour, kegs of treacle, tins of tea and every possible thing we could store in her hold.

Two days after that we had all in readiness for our departure.

On this voyage Jip begged so hard to be taken that the Doctor finally gave in and said he could come. Polynesia and Chee-Chee were the only other animals to go with us. Dab-Dab was left in charge of the house and the animal family we were to leave behind.

At the river-wall we found a great crowd waiting to see us off.

Standing right near the gang-plank were my mother and father. I hoped that they would not make a scene, or burst into tears or anything like that. But as a matter of fact they behaved quite well – for parents. My mother said something about being sure not to get my feet wet; and my father just smiled a crooked sort of smile, patted me on the back and wished me luck. Good-byes are awfully uncomfortable things and I was glad when it was over and we passed on to the ship.

At last, after much pulling and tugging, we got the anchor up and undid a lot of mooring-ropes. Then the *Curlew* began to move gently down the river with the out-running tide, while the people on the wall cheered and waved their handkerchiefs.

For me indeed it was a great and wonderful feeling, that getting out into the open sea, when at length we passed the little lighthouse at the mouth of the river and found ourselves free of the land. It was all so new and different: just the sky above you and sea below. This ship, which was to be our house and our street, our home and our garden, for so many days to come, seemed so tiny in all this wide water – so tiny and yet so snug, sufficient, safe.

I looked around me and took in a deep breath. The Doctor was at the wheel steering the boat which was now leaping and plunging gently through the waves. (I had expected to feel sea-

Swearing to herself because she couldn't read the figures

sick at first but was delighted to find that I didn't.) Chee-Chee was coiling up ropes in the stern and laying them in neat piles. My work was fastening down the things on the deck so that nothing could roll about if the weather should grow rough when we got farther from the land. Jip was up in the peak of the boat with ears cocked and nose stuck out – like a statue, so still – his keen old eyes keeping a sharp look-out for floating wrecks, sand-bars and other dangers. Each one of us had some special job to do, part of the proper running of a ship. Even old Polynesia was taking the sea's temperature with the Doctor's bath-thermometer tied on the end of a string, to make sure there were no icebergs near us. As I listened to her swearing softly to herself because she couldn't read the pesky figures in the fading light, I realized that the voyage had begun in earnest and that very soon it would be night – my first night at sea!

THE SILVER FIDGIT

DURING the long period on our trip to Spidermonkey Island the Doctor became interested again in his study of the languages of shellfish.

We were sailing right through great quantities of stuff that looked like dead grass. The Doctor told me this was gulf-weed. A little farther on it became so thick that it covered all the water as far as the eye could reach; it made the *Curlew* look as though she were moving across a meadow instead of sailing the Atlantic.

Crawling about upon this weed, crabs were to be seen. The Doctor fished several of these crabs up with a net and put them in his listening-tank to see if he could understand them. Among the crabs he also caught a strange-looking, chubby, little fish which he told me was called a Silver Fidgit.

After he had listened to the crabs for a while with no success, he put the fidgit into the tank and began to listen to that. I had to leave him at this moment to go and attend to some duties on the deck. But presently I heard him below shouting for me to come down again.

'Stubbins,' he cried as soon as he saw me, 'a most extraordinary thing! Quite unbelievable – I'm not sure whether I'm dreaming. Can't believe my own senses. I – I – I –'

'Why, Doctor,' I said, 'what is it? – What's the matter?'

'The fidgit,' he whispered, pointing with a trembling finger to the listening tank in which the little round fish was still swimming quietly, 'he talks English! And – and – *and he whistles tunes* – English tunes!'

'Talks English!' I cried. 'Whistles! – Why, it's impossible.'

'It's a fact,' said the Doctor, white in the face with excitement. 'It's only a few words, scattered, with no particular sense to them – all mixed up with his own language which I can't make out yet. But they're English words, unless there's something very wrong with my hearing. And the tune he whistles, it's as plain as anything – always the same tune. Now you listen and tell me what you make of it. Tell me everything you hear. Don't miss a word.'

I went to the glass tank upon the table while the Doctor grabbed a notebook and a pencil. Undoing my collar I stood upon the empty packing-case he had been using for a stand and put my right ear down under the water.

For some moments I detected nothing at all – except, with my dry ear, the heavy breathing of the Doctor as he waited, all stiff and anxious, for me to say something. At last from within the water, sounding like a child singing miles and miles away, I heard an unbelievably thin, small voice.

'Ah!' I said.

'What is it?' asked the Doctor in a hoarse, trembly whisper. 'What does he say?'

'I can't quite make it out,' I said. 'It's mostly in some strange fish language – Oh, but wait a minute! – Yes, now I get it – "No smoking" ... "My, here's a queer one!" "Popcorn and picture postcards here" ... "This way out" ... "Don't spit" – What funny things to say, Doctor! – Oh, but wait! – Now he's whistling the tune.'

'What tune is it?' gasped the Doctor.

'John Peel.'

'Ah hah,' cried the Doctor, 'that's what I made it out to be.' And he wrote furiously in his notebook.

I went on listening.

'This is most extraordinary,' the Doctor kept muttering to himself as his pencil went wiggling over the page. 'Most extraordinary – but frightfully thrilling. I wonder where he – '

'Here's some more,' I cried, 'some more English ... "*The big tank needs cleaning*" ... That's all. Now he's talking fish talk again.'

'The big tank!' the Doctor murmured, frowning in a puzzled kind of way. 'I wonder where on earth he learned –'

Then he bounded up out of his chair.

'I have it,' he yelled; 'this fish has escaped from an aquarium. Why, of course! Look at the kind of things he has learned: "Picture postcards" – they always sell them in aquariums; "Don't spit"; "No smoking"; "This way out" – the things the attendants say. And then, "My, here's a queer one!" That's the kind of thing that people exclaim when they look into the tanks. It all fits. There's no doubt about it, Stubbins: we have here a fish who has escaped from captivity. And it's quite possible – not certain, by any means, but quite possible – that I may now, through him, be able to establish communication with the shellfish. This is a great piece of luck.'

A little after midnight I fell asleep in a chair; and for five hours the *Curlew* was allowed to drift where she liked. But still John Dolittle worked on, trying his hardest to understand the fidgit's language, struggling to make the fidgit understand him.

When I woke up it was broad daylight again. The Doctor was still standing at the listening-tank, looking as tired as an owl and dreadfully wet. But on his face there was a proud and happy smile.

'Stubbins,' he said as soon as he saw me stir, 'I've done it. I've got the key to the fidgit's language. It's a frightfully difficult language – quite different from anything I ever heard. The only thing it reminds me of – slightly – is ancient Hebrew. It isn't shellfish; but it's a big step towards it. Now, the next thing, I want you to take a pencil and a fresh notebook and write down everything I say. The fidgit has agreed to answer some very important questions. I will translate it into English and put it down in the book. Are you ready?'

Once more the Doctor lowered his ear beneath the level of the water and, as he began to speak, I started to write.

THE DOCTOR: 'Is there any part of the sea deeper than that known as the Nero Deep – I mean the one near the Island of Guam?'

THE FIDGIT: 'Why, certainly. There's one much deeper than that near the mouth of the Amazon River. But it's small and hard to find. We call it "The Deep Hole". And there's another in the Antarctic Sea.'

THE DOCTOR: 'I am most anxious to get down to the bottom of the sea – to study many things. But we land animals, as you no doubt know, are unable to breathe under water. Have you any ideas that might help me?'

THE FIDGIT: 'I think that for both your difficulties the best thing for you would be to try and get hold of the Great Glass Sea Snail.'

THE DOCTOR: 'Er – who, or what, is the Great Glass Sea Snail?'

THE FIDGIT: 'He is an enormous salt-water snail, one of the winkle family, but as large as a big house. He can go to any part of the ocean, at all depths, because he doesn't have to be afraid of any creature in the sea. His shell is made of transparent mother-o'-pearl so that you can see through it; but it's thick and strong. When he is out of his shell and he carries it empty on his back, there is room in it for a wagon and a pair of horses.'

THE DOCTOR: 'I feel that that is just the creature I have been looking for. He could take me and my assistant inside his shell and we could explore the deepest depths in safety. Do you think you could get him for me?'

THE FIDGIT: 'Alas! no. I would willingly if I could; but he is hardly ever seen by ordinary fish. He lives at the bottom of the Deep Hole, and seldom comes out – And into the Deep Hole, the lower waters of which are muddy, fishes such as we are afraid to go.'

THE DOCTOR: 'Dear me! That's a terrible disappointment. Are there many of this kind of snail in the sea?'

THE FIDGIT: 'Oh, no. He is the last of the Giant Shellfish. He belongs to past ages when the whales were land animals and all that. They say he is over seventy thousand years old.'

THE DOCTOR: 'Good gracious, what wonderful things he could tell me! I do wish I could meet him.'

THE FIDGIT: 'Were there any more questions you wished to

'He is an enormous salt-water snail'

ask me? This water in your tank is getting quite warm and sickly. I'd like to be put back into the sea as soon as you can spare me.'

THE DOCTOR: 'Well, that is all, I think. I hate to put you back into the sea, because I know that as soon as I do, I'll think of a hundred other questions I wanted to ask you. But I must keep my promise. Would you care for anything before you go? – It seems a cold day – some cracker-crumbs or something?'

THE FIDGIT: 'No, I won't stop. All I want at present is fresh sea-water.'

THE DOCTOR: 'I cannot thank you enough for all the information you have given me. You have been very helpful and patient.'

THE FIDGIT: 'Pray do not mention it. It has been a real pleasure to be of assistance to the great John Dolittle. You are, as of course you know, already quite famous among the better class of fishes. Good-bye!– and good luck to you, to your ship and to all your plans!'

The Doctor carried the listening-tank to a porthole, opened it and emptied the tank into the sea.

'Good-bye!' he murmured as a faint splash reached us from without.

I dropped my pencil on the table and leaned back with a sigh. My fingers were so stiff with writer's cramp that I felt as though I should never be able to open my hand again. But I, at least, had had a night's sleep. As for the poor Doctor, he was so weary that he had hardly put the tank back upon the table and dropped into a chair, when his eyes closed and he began to snore.

I put the notebook carefully in a drawer and went on deck to take the wheel.

BAD WEATHER

ONE day after we had been at sea for many weeks, I noticed something peculiar. We were not going as fast as we had been. Our favourable wind had almost entirely disappeared. The *Curlew* just dawdled along at the speed of a toddling babe.

I now saw that the Doctor was becoming uneasy. He kept getting out his sextant (an instrument which tells you what part of the ocean you are in) and making calculations.

'But, Doctor,' I said when I found him one afternoon mumbling to himself about the misty appearance of the sky, 'it wouldn't matter so much, would it, if we did take a little longer over the trip? We've got plenty to eat on board; and the Purple

He kept getting out his sextant

Bird-of-Paradise will know that we have been delayed by something that we couldn't help.'

'Yes, I suppose so,' he said thoughtfully. 'But I hate to keep her waiting. At this season of the year she generally goes to the Peruvian mountains – for her health. Ah, here comes a wind – not very strong – but maybe it'll grow.'

A gentle breeze from the north-east came singing through the ropes; and we smiled up hopefully at the *Curlew*'s leaning masts.

'We've only got another hundred and fifty miles to make, to

sight the coast of Brazil,' said the Doctor. 'If that wind would just stay with us, steady, for a full day we'd see land.'

But suddenly the wind changed, swung to the east, then back to the north-east – then to the north. It came in fitful gusts, as though it hadn't make up its mind which way to blow; and I was kept busy at the wheel, swinging the *Curlew* this way and that to keep the right side of it.

Presently we heard Polynesia, who was in the rigging keeping a lookout for land or passing ships, screech down to us:

'Bad weather coming. That jumpy wind is an ugly sign. And look! – over there in the east – see that black line, low down? If that isn't a storm I'm a land-lubber. The gales round here are fierce when they do blow – tear your canvas out like paper. You take the wheel, Doctor: it'll need strong arms if it's a real storm. I'll go wake Jip and Chee-Chee. This looks bad to me. We'd best get all the sail down right away, till we see how strong she's going to blow.'

I must confess I was frightened. You see I had only so far seen the sea in friendly moods; sometimes quiet and lazy; sometimes laughing, venturesome and reckless; sometimes brooding and poetic, when moonbeams turn her ripples into silver threads and dreaming snowy nightclouds piled up fairy-castles in the sky. But as yet I had not known, or even guessed at, the terrible strength of the sea's wild anger.

When that storm finally struck us we leaned right over flatly on our side, as though some invisible giant had slapped the poor *Curlew* on the cheek.

After that things happened so thick and so fast that what with the wind that stopped your breath, the driving, blinding water, the deafening noise and the rest, I haven't a very clear idea of how our shipwreck came about.

I remember seeing the sails, which we were now trying to roll up upon the deck, torn out of our hands by the wind and go overboard like a penny balloon – very nearly carrying Chee-Chee with them. And I have a dim recollection of Polynesia screeching somewhere for one of us to go downstairs and close the portholes.

In spite of our masts being bare we were now scudding along to the southward at a great pace. But every once in a while huge grey-black waves would arise from under the ship's side like nightmare monsters, swell and climb, then crash down upon us, pressing us into the sea; and the poor *Curlew* would come to a standstill, half under water, like a gasping, drowning pig.

While I was clambering along towards the wheel to see the Doctor, clinging like a leech with hands and legs to the rails lest I be blown overboard, one of these tremendous seas tore loose my hold, filled my throat with water and swept me like a cork the full length of the deck. My head struck a door with an awful bang. And then I fainted.

When I awoke I was very hazy in my head. The sky was blue and the sea was calm. At first I thought I must have fallen asleep in the sun on the deck of the *Curlew*. And thinking that I would be late for my turn at the wheel, I tried to rise to my feet. I found I couldn't; my arms were tied to something behind me with a piece of rope. By twisting my neck around I found this to be a mast, broken off short. Then I realized that I wasn't sitting on a ship at all. I was only sitting on a piece of one. I began to feel uncomfortably scared. Screwing up my eyes, I searched the rim of the sea north, east, south and west: no land; no ships; nothing was in sight. I was alone in the ocean!

At last, little by little, my bruised head hurt less and I began to remember what had happened. Working my hand into my pocket, I found my penknife and cut the rope that tied me. This reminded me of a shipwreck story which Joe had once told me, of a captain who had tied his son to a mast in order that he shouldn't be washed overboard by the gale. So of course it must have been the Doctor who had done the same to me.

But where was he? And where were the others?

The awful thought came to me that the Doctor and the rest of them must be drowned, since there was no other wreckage to be seen upon the waters. I got to my feet and stared around the sea again. Nothing – nothing but water and sky!

Presently a long way off I saw the small dark shape of a bird skimming low down over the swell. When it came quite close I saw it was a Stormy Petrel. Twice it circled round my raft, lazily, with hardly a flip of the wing. And then it went off in the direction from which it had come. And I was alone once more.

I found I was somewhat hungry – and a little thirsty too. I began to think all sorts of miserable thoughts, the way one does when one is lonesome and has missed breakfast. What was going to become of me now, if the Doctor and the rest were drowned? I would starve to death or die of thirst.

I went on like this for a while, growing gloomier and gloomier, when suddenly I thought of Polynesia. 'You're always safe with the Doctor,' she had said. 'He gets there. Remember that.'

I'm sure I wouldn't have minded so much if he had been here with me. It was this being all alone that made me uneasy. But if what Polynesia had said was true, he couldn't be drowned and things would come out all right in the end somehow.

I threw out my chest, buttoned up my collar and began walking up and down the short raft to keep warm. I would be like John Dolittle. I wouldn't cry – and I wouldn't get excited.

How long I paced back and forth I don't know. But it was a long time – for I had nothing else to do.

At last I got tired and lay down to rest. And in spite of all my troubles, I soon fell fast asleep.

'Are you awake?' said a high silvery voice at my elbow.

I sprang up as though someone had stuck a pin in me. And there, perched at the very end of my raft, her beautiful golden tail glowing dimly in the starlight, sat Miranda, the Purple Bird-of-Paradise!

Never have I been so glad to see anyone in my life. I almost fell into the water as I leapt to hug her.

'I didn't want to wake you,' said she. 'I guessed you must be tired after all you've been through. Don't squash the life out of me, boy: I'm not a stuffed duck, you know.'

'Oh, Miranda, you dear old thing,' said I, 'I'm so glad to see you. Tell me, where is the Doctor? Is he alive?'

'Of course he's alive – and it's my firm belief he always will be. He's over there, about forty miles to the westward.'

'Are you awake?' said a high silvery voice at my elbow

'What's he doing there?'

'He's sitting on the other half of the *Curlew* shaving himself – or he was, when I left him.'

'Well, thank heaven he's alive!' said I. 'And the animals, are they all right?'

'Yes, they're with him. Your ship broke in half in the storm. The Doctor had tied you down when he found you stunned. And the part you were on got separated and floated away. Golly, it *was* a storm! It was the petrel that first gave us the tip where you were.'

'Well, but how can I get to the Doctor, Miranda? – I haven't any oars.'

'Get to him! – Why, your'e going to him now. Look behind you.'

I turned around. The moon was just rising on the sea's edge. And I now saw that my raft was moving through the water, but so gently that I had not noticed it before.

'What's moving us?' I asked.

'Some porpoises,' said Miranda.

I went to the back of the raft and looked down into the water. And just below the surface I could see the dim forms of four big porpoises, their sleek skins glinting in the moonlight, pushing at the raft with their noses.

'They're old friends of the Doctor's,' said Miranda. 'They'd do anything for John Dolittle.'

Presently from somewhere in the murky dusk I heard Polynesia singing a sailor's song – just as though she were back at Puddleby in the warm kitchen by the fireside. And in a little, by peering and peering in the direction of the sound, I at last made out a dim mass of tattered, splintered wreckage – all that remained of the poor *Curlew* floating low down upon the water.

A hulloa came through the night. And I answered it. We kept it up, calling to one another back and forth across the calm night sea. And a few minutes later the two halves of our brave little ruined ship bumped gently together again.

Close down to the edge of the water, using the sea's calm surface for a mirror and a piece of broken bottle for a razor, John Dolittle was shaving his face by the light of the moon.

LAND!

THEY all gave me a great greeting as I clambered off my half of the ship on to theirs. The Doctor brought me a wonderful drink of fresh water which he drew from a barrel; and Chee-Chee and Polynesia stood around me feeding me ship's biscuit.

But it was the sight of the Doctor's smiling face – just knowing that I was with him once again – that cheered me more than anything else. Just to be with him gave you a wonderful feeling of comfort and safety.

Except for his appearance (his clothes were crumpled and damp and his battered high hat was stained with salt water) that storm which had so terrified me had disturbed him no more than bumping into me on the Oventhorpe Road that rainy night months ago.

Politely thanking Miranda for getting me so quickly, he asked her if she would now go ahead of us and show us the way to Spidermonkey Island. Next, he gave orders to the porpoises to leave my old piece of the ship and push the bigger half wherever the Bird-of-Paradise should lead us.

How much he had lost in the wreck besides his razor I did not know – everything, most likely, together with all the money he owned. And still he was smiling as though he wanted for nothing in the world. The only things he had saved, as far as I could see – beyond the barrel of water and bag of biscuit – were his precious notebooks. These, I saw when he stood up, he had strapped around his waist with yards and yards of twine.

The only inconvenience we suffered from was the cold. This seemed to increase as we went forward. The Doctor said that the island, disturbed from its usual paths by the great gale, had evidently drifted farther south than it had ever been before.

On the third night poor Miranda came back to us nearly frozen. She told the Doctor that in the morning we would find the island quite close to us, though we couldn't see it now as it was a misty dark night. She said that she must hurry back at once to a warmer climate; and that she would visit the Doctor in Puddleby next August as usual.

After the Doctor had thanked her again and again for all that she had done for us, she wished us good luck and disappeared into the night.

We were all awake early in the morning, long before it was light, waiting for our first glimpse of the country we had come so far to see. And as the rising sun turned the eastern sky to grey, of course it was old Polynesia who first shouted that she could see palm-trees and mountain tops.

The porpoises gave us one last push and our strange-looking craft bumped gently on a low beach. Then, thanking our lucky stars for a chance to stretch our cramped legs, we all bundled off on to the land – the first land, even though it was floating land, that we had trodden for six weeks. What a thrill I felt as I realized that Spidermonkey Island, the little spot in the atlas which my pencil had touched, lay at last beneath my feet!

When the light increased still further we noticed that the palms and grasses of the island seemed withered and almost dead. The Doctor said that it must be on account of the cold that the island was now suffering from in its new climate. These trees and grasses, he told us, were the kind that belonged to warm, tropical weather.

As we were preparing to go inland and explore the island, we suddenly noticed a whole band of Red Indians watching us with great curiosity from among the trees. The Doctor went forward to talk to them. He tried by signs to show them that he had come on a friendly visit. The Indians didn't seem to like us however. They evidently wanted us to leave the island at once. It was a very uncomfortable situation.

At last the Doctor made them understand that he only wanted to see the island all over and that then he would go away – though how he meant to do it, with no boat to sail in, was more than I could imagine.

While they were talking among themselves another Indian arrived – apparently with a message that they were wanted in some other part of the island. Because presently, shaking their spears threateningly at us, they went off with the newcomer.

'They're going off to their village,' said Polynesia. 'I'll bet there's a village on the other side of those mountains. If you take my advice, Doctor, you'll get away from this beach while their backs are turned. They may grow friendlier when they see we mean no harm. They have honest, open faces and look like a decent crowd to me. They're just ignorant – probably never saw white folks before.'

So, feeling a little bit discouraged by our first reception, we moved off towards the mountains in the centre of the island.

Polynesia and Chee-Chee were good guides and splendid jungle-hunters; and the two of them set to work at once looking for food for us. In a very short space of time they had found quite a number of different fruits and nuts which made excellent eating, though none of us knew the names of any of them. We discovered a nice clean stream of good water which came down from the mountains; so we were supplied with something to drink as well.

We followed the stream up towards the heights. And presently we came to parts where the woods were thinner and the ground rocky and steep. Here we could get glimpses of wonderful views all over the island, with the blue sea beyond.

While we were admiring one of these the Doctor suddenly said, 'Sh! – A Jabizri! – Don't you hear it?'

We listened and heard, somewhere in the air about us, an extraordinary musical hum – like a bee, but not just one note. This hum rose and fell, up and down – almost like someone singing.

'No other insect but the Jabizri beetle hums like that,' said the Doctor. 'I wonder where he is – quite near, by the sound – flying among the trees probably. Oh, look! There he goes!'

A huge beetle, easily three inches long I should say, suddenly flew by our noses. The Doctor got frightfully excited. He took off his hat to use as a net, swooped at the beetle and caught it. From his pocket he brought out a glass-topped box, and into this he very skilfully made the beetle walk from under the rim of the hat. Then he rose up happy as a child, to examine his new treasure through the glass lid.

It certainly was a most beautiful insect. It was pale blue underneath; but its back was glossy black with huge red spots on it.

'There isn't an entymologist in the whole world who wouldn't give all he has to be in my shoes today,' said the Doctor. 'Hulloa! This Jabizri's got something on his leg. Doesn't look like mud. I wonder what it is.'

He took the beetle carefully out of the box and held it by its

He took off his hat and caught it

back in his fingers, where it waved its six legs slowly in the air. We all crowded about him peering at it. Rolled around the middle section of its right foreleg was something that looked like a thin dried leaf. It was bound on very neatly with strong spider-web.

It was marvellous to see how John Dolittle with his fat heavy fingers undid that cobweb cord and unrolled the leaf, whole, without tearing it or hurting the precious beetle. The Jabizri he put back into the box. Then he spread the leaf out flat and examined it.

For several moments there was a dead silence while we all stared at the leaf, fascinated and mystified.

'I think this is written in blood,' said the Doctor at last. 'It turns that colour when it's dry. Somebody pricked his finger to makes these pictures. It's an old dodge when you're short of ink – but highly unsanitary. What an extraordinary thing to find tied to a beetle's leg! I wish I could talk beetle-language, and find out where the Jabizri got it from.'

'But what is it?' I asked. 'Rows of little pictures and signs. What do you make of it, Doctor?'

'It's a letter,' he said, 'a picture-letter.'

Then he fell to muttering over the pictures.

All of a sudden the Doctor looked up sharply at me, a wonderful smile of delighted understanding spreading over his face.

'*Long Arrow!*' he cried. 'Don't you see, Stubbins? – Why, of course! Only a naturalist would think of doing a thing like this: giving his letter to a beetle – not to a common beetle, but to the rarest of all, one that other naturalists would try to catch. Well, well! Long Arrow! – A picture-letter from Long Arrow. For pictures are the only writing that he knows.'

'Yes, but who is the letter to?' I asked.

'It's to me very likely. Miranda had told him, I know, years ago, that some day I meant to come here. But if not for me, then it's for anyone who caught the beetle and read it. It's a letter to the world.'

'Well, but what does it say? It doesn't seem to me that it's much good to you now you've got it.'

'Yes, it is,' he said, 'because, look, I can read it now. First picture: men walking up a mountain – that's Long Arrow and his party; men going into a hole in a mountain – they enter a cave looking for medicine-plants or mosses; a mountain falling down – some hanging rocks must have slipped and trapped them, imprisoned them in the cave. And this was the only living creature that could carry a message for them to the outside world – a beetle, who could burrow his way into the open air. Now look at the next picture: men pointing to their open mouths – they are hungry; men praying – begging anyone who

The Jabizri's mysterious picture-letter

finds this letter to come to their assistance; men lying down – they are sick, or starving. This letter, Stubbins, is their last cry for help.'

He sprang to his feet as he ended, snatched out a notebook and put the letter between the leaves. His hands were trembling with haste and agitation.

'Come on!' he cried. 'Up the mountain – all of you. There's not a moment to lose. Stubbins, bring the water and nuts with you. Heaven only knows how long they've been pining underground. Let's hope and pray we're not too late!'

'But where are you going to look?' I asked.

'Didn't you see the first picture?' he said, grabbing up his hat from the ground and cramming it on his head. 'It was an oddly shaped mountain – looked like a hawk's head. Well, there's where he is – if he's still alive. First thing for us to do, is to get up on a high peak and look around the island for a mountain shaped like a hawk's head. Come on! Hurry! To delay may mean death to the greatest naturalist ever born!'

HAWK'S HEAD MOUNTAIN

WHEN we had scrambled to the top of a high peak, almost instantly we saw the strange mountain pictured in the letter. In shape it was the perfect image of a hawk's head, and was, as far as we could see, the second highest summit in the island.

With one look at the sun for direction, down the Doctor dashed again taking all the short cuts. For a fat man, he was certainly the swiftest cross-country runner I ever saw.

I floundered after him as fast as I could. Jip, Chee-Chee and Polynesia were a long way ahead – even beyond the Doctor – enjoying the hunt like a paper-chase.

When we reached the foot of the mountain the Doctor said:

'Now we will separate and search for caves. If anyone finds anything like a cave or a hole where the earth and rocks have fallen in, he must shout and hulloa to the rest of us. If we find nothing we will all gather here in about an hour's time. Everybody understand?'

Then we all went off our different ways.

Each of us, you may be sure, was anxious to be the one to make a discovery. And never was a mountain searched so thoroughly. But alas! nothing could we find that looked in the least like a fallen-in cave.

One by one, tired and disappointed, we straggled back to the meeting-place. The Doctor seemed gloomy and impatient but by no means inclined to give up.

He was the swiftest cross-country runner I ever saw

'Polynesia,' asked the Doctor, 'did you see *nothing* that might put us on the right track?'

'Not a thing, Doctor – but I have a plan.'

'Oh, good!' cried John Dolittle, full of hope renewed. 'What is it? Let's hear it.'

'You still have that beetle with you,' she asked; 'the Biz-biz, or whatever it is you call the wretched insect?'

'Yes,' said the Doctor, producing the glass-topped box from his pocket, 'here it is.'

'All right. Now listen,' said she. 'If what you have supposed is true – that is, that Long Arrow had been trapped inside the mountain by falling rock, he probably found that beetle inside the cave – perhaps many other different beetles too, eh? He wouldn't have been likely to take the Biz-biz in with him, would he? – He was hunting plants, you say, not beetles. Isn't that right?'

'Yes,' said the Doctor, 'that's probably so.'

'All right. Then the thing to do is to let the beetle go – and watch him; and sooner or later he'll return to his home in Long Arrow's cave. And there we will follow him – or at all events,' she added, smoothing down her wing-feathers with a very superior air, 'we will follow him till the miserable bug starts nosing under the earth. But at least he will show us what part of the mountain Long Arrow is hidden in.'

'But he may fly, if I let him out,' said the Doctor. 'Then we shall just lose him and be no better off than we were before.'

'*Let* him fly,' snorted Polynesia scornfully. 'A parrot can wing it as fast as a Biz-biz, I fancy. If he takes to the air, I'll guarantee not to let the little devil out of my sight.'

'Splendid!' cried the Doctor. 'Polynesia, you have a great brain. I'll set him to work at once and see what happens.'

Again we all clustered round the Doctor as he carefully lifted off the glass lid and let the big beetle climb out upon his finger.

'Doctor,' said Polynesia, 'why not tie another message to the creature's leg, telling Long Arrow that we're doing our best to reach him and that he mustn't give up hope?'

'I will,' said the Doctor. And in a minute he had pulled a dry leaf from a bush near by and was covering it with little pictures in pencil.

At last, neatly fixed up with his new mail-bag, Mr Jabizri crawled off the Doctor's finger to the ground and looked about him. He stretched his legs, polished his nose with his front feet, and then moved off leisurely to the westward.

We had expected him to walk *up* the mountain; instead, he walked *around* it. Do you know how long it takes a beetle to walk round a mountain? Well, I assure you it takes an unbelievably long time. As the hours dragged by, we hoped and hoped that he would get up and fly the rest, and let Polynesia carry on the work of following him. But he never opened his wings once.

After he had led us the whole way round the mountain he brought us to the exact spot where we started from and there he came to a dead stop.

'Well,' said Polynesia, 'a lot of good that trip was. He doesn't even have enough sense to go home.'

'Maybe he just wanted some exercise,' said Jip. 'Wouldn't you want to stretch your legs if you'd been shut up in a box all day? Probably his home is near here, and that's why he's come back.'

'But why,' I asked, 'did he go the whole way round the mountain first?'

Then Chee-Chee, Polynesia, Jip and I sat down to rest. Suddenly the Doctor called out.

'Look, look!'

We turned and found that he was pointing to the Jabizri, who was now walking *up* the mountain at a much faster and more businesslike gait.

'Well,' said Jip, 'if he is going to walk *over* the mountain and back, for more exercise, I'll wait for him here. Chee-Chee and Polynesia can follow him.'

Indeed it would have taken a monkey or a bird to climb the place which the beetle was now walking up. It was a smooth, flat part of the mountain-side, steep as a wall.

But presently, when the Jibizri was no more than ten feet above our heads, we all cried out together. For, even while we watched him, he had disappeared into the face of the rock like a raindrop soaking into sand.

'He's gone,' cried Polynesia.' There must be a hole up there.' And in a twinkling she had fluttered up the rock and was clinging to the face of it with her claws.

'Yes,' she shouted down, 'we've run him to earth at last. His hole is right here, behind a patch of lichen – big enough to get two fingers in.'

'Ah,' cried the Doctor, 'this great slab of rock then must have slid down from the summit and shut off the mouth of the cave like a door. Poor fellows! What a dreadful time they must have spent in there! I wonder how thick it is,' and he picked up a big stone and banged it with all his might against the face of the rock. It made a hollow booming sound, like a giant drum. We all stood still listening while the echo of it died slowly away.

And then a cold shiver ran down my spine. For, from within the mountain, back came three answering knocks: *Boom! ... Boom! ... Boom!*

Wide-eyed we looked at one another as though the earth itself had spoken. And the solemn little silence that followed was broken by the Doctor.

'Thank heaven,' he said in a hushed reverent voice, 'some of them at least are alive!'

A GREAT MOMENT

THE next part of our problem was the hardest of all: how to roll aside, pull down or break open, that gigantic slab. As we gazed up at it towering above our heads, it looked indeed a hopeless task for our tiny strength.

Chee-Chee scaled up the sheer wall of the slab and examined the top of it where it leaned against the mountain-side; I uprooted bushes and stripped off hanging creepers that might conceal a weak place; the Doctor got more leaves and composed new picture-letters for the Jabizri to take in if he should turn up again; whilst Polynesia carried up a handful of nuts and pushed them into the beetle's hole, one by one, for the prisoners inside to eat.

'Nuts are so nourishing,' she said.

But Jip it was who, scratching at the foot of the slab like a good ratter, made the discovery which led to our final success.

'Doctor,' he cried, running up to John Dolittle with his nose all covered with black mud, 'this slab is resting on nothing but a bed of soft earth. If we can only scratch the earth-bed away from under, the slab might drop a little. Then maybe the Indians can climb out over the top.'

The Doctor hurried to examine the place where Jip had dug.

'Why, yes,' he said. 'if we can get the earth away from under this front edge, the slab is standing up so straight, we might even make it fall right down in this direction. It's well worth trying. Let's get at it, quick.'

We had no tools but the sticks and slivers of stone which we could find around. A strange sight we must have looked, the whole crew of us squatting down on our heels, scratching and burrowing at the foot of the mountain, like five badgers in a row.

After about an hour, during which in spite of the cold the sweat fell from our foreheads in all directions, the Doctor said,

'Be ready to jump from under, clear out of the way, if she shows signs of moving. If this slab falls on anybody, it will squash him flatter than a pancake.'

Presently there was a grating, grinding sound.

'Look out!' yelled John Dolittle. 'Here she comes! – Scatter!'

We ran for our lives, outwards, towards the sides. The big rock slid gently down and as I looked upwards, I saw the top coming very slowly away from the mountain-side. We had unbalanced it below. Faster and faster the top swung forward, downward. Then, with a roaring crash which shook the whole mountain-range beneath our feet, it struck the earth and cracked in halves.

The gloomy black mouth of a tunnel, full twenty feet high, was revealed. In the centre of this opening stood an enormous Red Indian, seven feet tall, handsome, muscular, slim and naked – but for a beaded cloth about his middle and an eagle's feather in his hair. He held one hand across his face to shield his eyes from the blinding sun which he had not seen in many days.

'It is he!' I heard the Doctor whisper at my elbow. 'I know him by his great height and the scar upon his chin.'

And he stepped forward slowly across the fallen stone with his hand outstretched to the red man.

Presently the Indian uncovered his eyes. And I saw that they

I saw the top coming very slowly away from the mountain-side

had a curious piercing gleam in them – like the eyes of an eagle, but kinder and more gentle. He slowly raised his right arm, the rest of him still and motionless like a statue, and took the Doctor's hand in his. It was a great moment. Polynesia nodded to me in a knowing, satisfied kind of way.

Then the Doctor tried to speak to Long Arrow. But the Indian knew no English, of course, and the Doctor knew no Indian. Presently, to my surprise, I heard the Doctor trying him in the language of eagles.

'Great Red-Skin,' he said in the fierce screams and short grunts that the big birds use, 'never have I been so glad in all my life as I am today to find you still alive.'

In a flash Long Arrow's stony face lit up with a smile of understanding; and back came the answer in eagle-tongue.

'Mighty White Man, I owe my life to you. For the remainder of my days I am your servant to command,' said Long Arrow.

Travellers who have since visited Spidermonkey Island tell me that the huge stone slab is now one of the regular sights of the island. And that the Indian guides, when showing it to visitors, always tell *their* story of how it came there. They say that when the Doctor found that the rocks had entrapped his friend, Long Arrow, he was so angry that he ripped the mountain in halves with his bare hands and let him out.

On the way to the village some Indians met us and told Long Arrow something which appeared to be sad news, for on hearing it, his face grew very grave. The Doctor asked him what was wrong. And Long Arrow said he had just been informed that the chief of the tribe, an old man of eighty, had died early that morning.

'That,' Polynesia whispered in my ear, 'must have been what they went back to the village for, when the messenger fetched them, from the beach. Remember?'

'What did he die of?' asked the Doctor.

'He died of cold,' said Long Arrow.

Indeed, now that the sun was setting, we were all shivering ourselves.

'This is a serious thing,' said the Doctor to me. 'The island is still in the grip of that wretched current flowing southward. We will have to look into this tomorrow. If nothing can be done about it, the Indians had better take to canoes and leave the island. The chance of being wrecked will be better than getting frozen to death in the ice-floes of the Antarctic.'

Presently we came over a saddle in the hills, and, looking downward on the far side of the island, we saw the village – a large cluster of grass huts and gaily coloured totem-poles close by the edge of the sea.

A large cluster of huts and totem-poles by the edge of the sea

'How artistic!' said the Doctor. 'Delightfully situated. What is the name of the village?'

'Popsipetel,' said Long Arrow. 'That is the name also of the tribe, The word signifies in Indian tongue, *The Men of The Moving Land*.'

As Long Arrow took us around the island we found that not only the plants and trees were suffering from the cold: the animal life was even in worse straits.

Everywhere shivering birds were to be seen, their feathers all fluffed out, gathering together for flight to summer lands. And many lay dead upon the ground. Going down to the shore, we watched land-crabs in large numbers taking to the sea to find some better home. While away to the south-east we could see many icebergs floating – a sign that we were now not far from the terrible region of the Antarctic.

As we were looking out to sea, we noticed our friends the porpoises jumping through the waves. The Doctor hailed them and they came inshore.

He asked them how far we were from the South Polar Continent.

About a hundred miles, they told him. And then they asked why he wanted to know.

'Because this floating island we are on,' said he, 'is drifting southward all the time in a current. It's an island that ordinarily belongs somewhere in the tropic zone – real sultry weather, sunstrokes and all that. If it doesn't stop going southward pretty soon everything on it is going to perish.'

'Well,' said the porpoises, 'then the thing to do is to get back into a warmer climate, isn't it?'

'Yes, but how?' said the Doctor. 'We can't *row* it back.'

'No,' said they, 'but whales could push it – if only you got enough of them.'

'What a splendid idea! – Whales, the very thing!' said the Doctor. 'Do you think you could get me some?'

'Why, certainly,' said the porpoises. 'We passed one herd of them out there, sporting about among the icebergs. We'll ask them to come over. And if they aren't enough, we'll try and hunt up some more. Better have plenty.'

'Thank you,' said the Doctor. 'You are very kind. By the way, do you happen to know how this island came to be a floating island? At least half of it, I notice, is made of stone. It is very odd that it floats at all, isn't it?'

'It is unusual,' they said. 'But the explanation is quite simple. It used to be a mountainous part of South America – an overhanging part – sort of an awkward corner, you might say. Way back in the glacial days, thousands of years ago, it broke off from the mainland; and by some curious accident the inside of it, which is hollow, got filled with air as it fell into the ocean. You can only see less than half of the island: the bigger half is under water. And in the middle of it, underneath, is a huge rock air-chamber, running right up inside the mountains. And that's what keeps it floating.'

'What a curious phenomenon,' said the Doctor. 'I must make a note of that.' And out came the everlasting notebook.

The porpoises went bounding off towards the icebergs. And not long after, we saw the sea heaving and frothing as a big herd of whales came towards us at full speed.

They certainly were enormous creatures; and there must have been a good two hundred of them.

'Here they are,' said the porpoises, poking their heads out of the water.

'Good!' said the Doctor. 'Now ask them if they will be so good as to go down to the far end of the island, put their noses against it and push it back near the coast of Southern Brazil.'

Then we lay down upon the beach and waited.

After about an hour the Doctor got up and threw a stick into the water. For a while this floated motionless. But soon we saw it begin to move gently down the coast.

'Ah!' said the Doctor. 'See that? – The island is going north at last. Thank goodness!'

The Doctor took out his watch, threw more sticks into the water and made a rapid calculation.

'Humph! – Fourteen and a half knots an hour,' he murmured – 'a very nice speed. It should take us about five days to get back near Brazil. Well, that's that. Quite a load off my mind. I declare I feel warmer already. Let's go and get something to eat.'

THE WHISPERING ROCKS

As usual, the doctor was kept busy caring for sick Popsipetel babies, monkeys with runny noses and all manner of ailments the animals and the people of the island brought to him to cure.

One day, when he had finished with all his patients, we went for a complete trip round the island's shores by canoe.

Shortly after we started, while still off the lower end of the island, we sighted a steep point on the coast where the sea was in a great state of turmoil, white with soapy froth. On going nearer, we found that this was caused by our friendly whales who were still faithfully working away with their noses against the end of the island, driving us northward.

Here and there we noticed that the trees on the shore already looked greener and more healthy. Spidermonkey Island was getting back into her home climate.

About halfway to Popsipetel we went ashore and spent two or three days exploring the central part of the island. Our Indian paddlers took us up into the mountains, very steep and high in this region, overhanging the sea. And they showed us what they called the Whispering Rocks.

This was a very peculiar and striking piece of scenery. It was like a great vast basin, or circus, in the mountains, and out of the centre of it there rose a table of rock with an ivory chair upon it.

We asked our guides why it was called the Whispering Rocks; and they said, 'Go down into it and we will show you.'

The great bowl was miles deep and miles wide. We scrambled down the rocks and they showed us how, even when you stood far, far apart from one another, you merely had to whisper in that great place and everyone in the theatre could hear you.

Our guides told us that it was here, in days long gone by when the Popsipetels owned the whole of Spidermonkey Island, that the kings were crowned.

They showed us also an enormous hanging stone perched on

Working away with their noses against the end of the island

the edge of a volcano's crater – the highest summit in the whole island. Although it was very far above us, we could see it quite plainly; and it looked wobbly enough to be pushed off its perch with the hand. There was a legend among the people, they said, that when the greatest of all Popsipetel kings should be crowned in the ivory chair, this hanging stone would tumble into the volcano's mouth and go straight down to the centre of the earth.

The Doctor said he would like to go and examine it closer.

And when we were come to the lip of the volcano (it took us half a day to get up to it) we found the stone was unbelievably large – big as a cathedral. Underneath it we could look right down into a black hole which seemed to have no bottom. The Doctor explained to us that volcanoes sometimes spurted up fire from these holes in their tops; but that those on floating islands were always cold and dead.

'Stubbins,' he said, looking up at the great stone towering above us, 'do you know what would most likely happen if that boulder should fall in?'

'No,' said I, 'what?'

'You remember the air-chamber which the porpoises told us lies under the centre of the island?'

'Yes.'

'Well, this stone is heavy enough, if it fell into the volcano, to break through into that air-chamber from above. And once it did, the air would escape and the floating island would float no more. It would sink.'

'But then everybody on it would be drowned, wouldn't they?' I asked.

'Oh, no, not necessarily, Stubbins. That would depend on the depth of the sea where the sinking took place. The island might touch bottom when it had only gone down, say, a hundred feet. But there would be lots of it sticking up above the water then, wouldn't there?'

'Yes,' I replied, 'I suppose there would.'

We returned to Popsipetel just as the dawn was breaking, and as soon as the Doctor had paid a visit to Long Arrow and seen that he was doing nicely, we proceeded to our own house at the far end of the village. Here we ate some breakfast and then lay down to take a good rest.

Rest, indeed, we needed; for life had been strenuous and busy for us ever since we had landed on the island. And it wasn't many minutes after our weary heads struck the pillows that the whole crew of us were sound asleep.

We were awakened by music. The glaring noonday sunlight was streaming in at our door, outside which some kind of a band appeared to be playing. We got up and looked out. Our house was surrounded by the whole population of Popsipetel. We were used to having quite a number of curious and admiring Indians waiting at our door at all hours; but this was quite different. The vast crowd was dressed in its best clothes. Bright beads, gaudy feathers and gay blankets gave cheerful colour to the scene. Everyone seemed in very good humour, singing or playing on musical instruments – mostly painted wooden whistles or drums made from skins.

We found Polynesia sitting on our door-post watching the show.

'The result of the election has just been announced,' said she. 'The name of the new chief was given out at noon.'

'And who is the new chief?' asked the Doctor.

'You are,' said Polynesia quietly.

'*I!*' gasped the Doctor. 'Well, of all things!'

'Yes,' said she, 'you're the one – and what's more, they've changed your surname for you. They didn't think that Dolittle was a proper or respectful name for a man who had done so much. So you are now to be known as Jong Thinkalot. How do you like it?'

'But I don't *want* to be a chief,' said the Doctor in an irritable voice.

'I'm afraid you'll have hard work to get out of it now,' said she, 'unless you're willing to put to sea again in one of their rickety canoes. You see you've been elected not merely the Chief of the Popsipetels; you're to be a king – the King of the whole of Spidermonkey Island.'

'Oh, Lord!' groaned the Doctor, 'I do wish they wouldn't be so enthusiastic! Bother it, I don't *want* to be a king!'

'I should think, Doctor,' said I, 'you'd feel rather proud and glad. I wish *I* had a chance to be a king.'

'Oh, I know it sounds grand,' said he, pulling on his boots miserably. 'But the trouble is, you can't take up responsibilities and then just drop them again when you feel like it. I have my own work to do. Scarcely one moment have I had to give to natural history since I landed on this island. I've been doing someone else's business all the time. And now they want me to go on doing it! Why, once I'm made King of the Popsipetels, that's the end of me as a useful naturalist. I'd be too busy for anything. All I'd be then is just a, er – er – just a king.'

'Look,' said Polynesia, 'here come the head men to announce your election. Hurry up and get your boots laced.'

The throng before our door had suddenly parted asunder, making a long lane; and down this we now saw a group of personages coming towards us. The man in front, a handsome old Indian with a wrinkled face, carried in his hands a wooden crown – a truly beautiful and gorgeous crown, even though of wood. Behind the old man came eight strong Indians bearing a litter.

When the old Indian told John Dolittle that he had come to take him to his coronation the Doctor politely begged to be excused from the honour, but the old man paid no attention.

'You are the chosen one,' said he. 'The people will have none but you.'

Into the Doctor's perplexed face suddenly there came a flash of hope.

'I'll go and see Long Arrow,' he whispered to me. 'Perhaps he will know of some way to get me out of this.'

And asking the personages to excuse him a moment, he left them there, standing at his door, and hurried off in the direction of Long Arrow's house. I followed him.

We found our big friend lying on a grass bed outside his home, where he had been moved that he might witness the holiday-making.

He carried in his hands a wooden crown

'Long Arrow,' said the Doctor speaking quickly in eagle-tongue so that the bystanders should not overhear, 'in dire peril I come to you for help. These men would make me their king. If such a thing befall me, all the great work I hoped to do must go undone, for who is there unfreer than a king? I pray you speak with them and persuade their kind well-meaning hearts that what they plan to do would be unwise.'

Long Arrow raised himself upon his elbow.

'O Kindly One,' said he (this seemed now to have become the usual manner of address when speaking to the Doctor), 'sorely it grieves me that the first wish you ask of me I should be unable to grant. Alas! I can do nothing. These people have so set their hearts on keeping you for king that if I tried to interfere they would drive me from their land and likely crown you in the end in any case. A king you must be, if only for a while. We must so arrange the business of governing that you may have time to give to Nature's secrets. Later we may be able to hit upon some plan to relieve you of the burden of the crown. But for now you must be king. These people are a headstrong tribe and they will have their way. There is no other course.'

Sadly the Doctor turned away from the bed and faced about. And there behind him stood the old man again, the crown still held in his wrinkled hands and the royal litter waiting at his elbow. With a deep reverence the bearers motioned towards the seat of the chair, inviting the white man to get in.

He turned back pleadingly again to Long Arrow in a last appeal for help. But the big Indian merely shook his head and pointed, like the bearers, to the waiting chair.

At last, almost in tears, John Dolittle stepped slowly into the litter and sat down. As he was hoisted on to the broad shoulders of the bearers I heard him still feebly muttering beneath his breath:

'Botheration take it! – I don't *want* to be a king!'

'Farewell!' called Long Arrow from his bed, 'and may good fortune ever stand within the shadow of your throne!'

'He comes! – He comes!' murmured the crowd. 'Away! Away! To the Whispering Rocks!'

And as the procession formed up to leave the village, the crowd about us began hurrying off in the direction of the mountains to make sure of good seats in the giant theatre where the crowning ceremony would take place.

THE CORONATION OF KING JONG

As Chee-Chee, Polynesia, Jip and I finally reached the dizzy edge of the great bowl and looked down inside it, it was like gazing over a never-ending ocean of copper-coloured faces; for every seat in the theatre was filled, every man, woman and child in the island – including Long Arrow who had been carried up on his sick bed – was there to see the show.

Soon we saw the royal litter, with the Doctor seated in it, slowly ascending the winding steps of the Table. Reaching the flat top at last, it halted and the Doctor stepped out upon a carpet of flowers. So still and perfect was the silence that even at that distance above I distinctly heard a twig snap beneath his tread.

Walking to the throne accompanied by the old Indian, the Doctor got up upon the stand and sat down. How tiny his little round figure looked when seen from that tremendous height! The throne had been made for longer-legged kings; and when he was seated his feet did not reach the ground but dangled six inches from the top step.

Then the old man turned round and looking up at the people began to speak in a quiet, even voice; but every word he said was easily heard in the farthest corner of the Whispering Rocks.

First he recited the names of all the great Popsipetel kings who in days long ago had been crowned in this ivory chair. He spoke of the greatness of the Popsipetel people, of their triumphs, of their hardships. Then waving his hand towards the Doctor he began recounting the things which this king-to-be had done. And I am bound to say that they easily outmatched the deeds of those who had gone before him.

At last the old man finished his speech and, stepping up to the chair, very respectfully removed the Doctor's battered high hat. He was about to put it upon the ground; but the Doctor took it from him hastily and kept it on his lap. Then taking up the Sacred Crown he placed it upon John Dolittle's head. It did not fit very well (for it had been made for smaller-headed kings), and, when the wind blew in freshly from the sunlit sea the Doctor had some difficulty in keeping it on. But it looked very splendid.

Turning once more to the people, the old man said:

'Men of Popsipetel, behold your elected king! – Are you content?'

And then at last the voice of the people broke loose.

'JONG! JONG!' they shouted. 'Long live KING JONG!'

The sound burst upon the solemn silence with the crash of a hundred cannon. There, where even a whisper carried miles, the shock of it was like a blow in the face.

Suddenly I saw the old man point upward, to the highest mountain in the island; and looking over my shoulder, I was just in time to see the Hanging Stone topple slowly out of sight – down into the heart of the volcano.

'See ye, Men of the Moving Land!' the old man cried. 'The stone has fallen and our legend has come true: the King of Kings is crowned this day!'

The Doctor too had seen the stone fall and he was now standing up looking at the sea expectantly.

'He's thinking of the air-chamber,' said Polynesia in my ear. 'Let us hope that the sea isn't very deep in these parts.'

After a full minute (so long did it take the stone to fall that depth) we heard a muffled, distant crunching thud – and then immediately after, a great hissing of escaping air. The Doctor, his face tense with anxiety, sat down in the throne again, still watching the blue water of the ocean with staring eyes.

Soon we felt the island slowly sinking beneath us. We saw the sea creep inland over the beaches as the shores went down – one foot, three feet, ten feet, twenty, fifty, a hundred. And then, thank goodness, gently as a butterfly alighting on a rose, it stopped! Spidermonkey Island had come to rest on the sandy bottom of the Atlantic, and earth was joined to earth once more.

Of course many of the houses near the shores were now under water. Popsipetel Village itself had entirely disappeared. But it didn't matter. No one was drowned; for every soul in the island was high up in the hills watching the coronation of King Jong.

In Popsipetel history the story was handed down (and it is firmly believed to this day) that when King Jong sat upon the throne, so great was his mighty weight, that the very island itself sank down to do him honour and never moved again.

THE SEA-SERPENT

LIFE in Spidermonkey Island went forward, month in month out, busily and pleasantly. The winter, with Christmas celebrations, came and went, and summer was with us once again before we knew it.

As time passed the Doctor became more and more taken up with the care of his big family; and the hours he could spare for his natural history work grew fewer and fewer. I knew that he often still thought of his house and garden in Puddleby and of his plans and ambitions; because once in a while we would notice his face grow thoughtful and a little sad, when something reminded him of England or his old life. But he never spoke of these things. And I truly believe he would have spent the remainder of his days on Spidermonkey Island if it hadn't been for an accident – and for Polynesia.

It was a perfect Popsipetel day, bright and hot, blue and yellow. Drowsily I looked out to sea, thinking of my mother and father. I wondered if they were getting anxious over my long absence. Beside me old Polynesia went on grumbling away in low steady tones; and her words began to mingle and mix with the gentle lapping of the waves upon the shore. It may have been the even murmur of her voice, helped by the soft and balmy air, that lulled me to sleep. I don't know. Anyhow I presently dreamed that the island had moved again – not floatingly as before, but suddenly, jerkily, as though something enormously powerful had heaved it up from its bed just once and let it down.

How long I slept after that I have no idea. I was awakened by a gentle pecking on the nose.

'Tommy! – Tommy!' (It was Polynesia's voice.) 'Wake *up*! – Gosh, what a boy, to sleep through an earthquake and never notice it! – Tommy, listen: here's our chance now. Wake *up*, for goodness' sake!'

'What's the matter?' I asked, sitting up with a yawn.

'Sh! – Look!' whispered Polynesia pointing out to sea.

Still only half awake, I stared before me with bleary, sleep-laden eyes. And in the shallow water, not more than thirty yards from shore, I saw an enormous pale-pink shell. Dome-shaped, it towered up in a graceful rainbow curve to a tremendous height; and round its base the surf broke gently in little waves of white. It could have belonged to the wildest dream.

'What in the world is it?' I asked.

'That,' whispered Polynesia, 'is what sailors for hundreds of years have called the *Sea-serpent*. I've seen it myself more than once from the decks of ships, at long range, curving in and out of the water. But now that I see it close and still, I very strongly suspect that the Sea-serpent of history is no other than the Great Glass Sea-Snail that the fidgit told us of. If that isn't the only fish of its kind in the seven seas, call me a carrion-crow. Tommy, we're in luck. Our job is to get the Doctor down here to look at that prize specimen before it moves off to the Deep Hole. If we can, then trust me, we may leave this blessed island yet. You stay here and keep an eye on it while I go after the Doctor. Don't move or speak – don't even breathe heavy: he might get scared – awful timid things, snails. Just watch him; and I'll be back in two shakes.'

It moved very little. From time to time it would try to draw itself up, the way a snail does when he goes to move, but almost at once it would sink down again as if exhausted. It seemed to me to act as though it were hurt underneath; but the lower part of it, which was below the level of the water, I could not see.

I was still absorbed in watching the great beast when Polynesia returned with the Doctor. They approached so silently

It moved very little

and so cautiously that I neither saw nor heard them coming till I found them crouching beside me on the sand.

One sight of the snail changed the Doctor completely. His eyes just sparkled with delight. I had not seen him so thrilled and happy since the time we caught the Jabizri beetle when we first landed on the island.

'It is he!' he whispered. 'The Great Glass Sea-Snail himself – not a doubt of it. Polynesia, go down the shore a way and see if you can find any of the porpoises for me. Perhaps they can tell us what the snail is doing here – it's very unusual for him to be

His eyes just sparkled with delight

in shallow water like this. And Stubbins, you go over to the harbour and bring me a small canoe. But be most careful how you paddle it round into this bay. If the snail should take fright and go out into the deeper water, we may never get a chance to see him again.'

'And don't tell any of the Indians,' Polynesia added in a whisper as I moved to go. 'We must keep this a secret or we'll have a crowd of sightseers round here in five minutes. It's mighty lucky we found the snail in a quiet bay.'

Reaching the harbour, I picked out a small light canoe from

among the number that were lying there and, without telling anyone what I wanted it for, got in and started off to paddle it down the shore.

Polynesia, I saw, when I rounded a rocky cape and came in sight of the bay, had got her errand done and returned ahead of me, bringing with her a pair of porpoises. These were already conversing in low tones with John Dolittle. I beached the canoe and went up to listen.

'What I want to know,' the Doctor was saying, 'is how the snail comes to be here. I was given to understand that he usually stayed in the Deep Hole: and that when he did come to the surface it was always in mid-ocean.'

'Oh, didn't you know? – Haven't you heard?' the porpoises replied. 'You covered up the Deep Hole when you sank the island. Why yes: you let it down right on top of the mouth of the Hole – sort of put the lid on, as it were. The fishes that were in it at the time have been trying to get out ever since. The Great Snail had the worst luck of all: the island nipped him by the tail just as he was leaving the Hole for a quiet evening stroll. And he was held there for six months trying to wriggle himself free. Finally he had to heave the whole island up at one end to get his tail loose. Didn't you feel a sort of an earthquake shock about an hour ago?'

'Yes, I did,' said the Doctor.

'Well, that was the snail heaving up the island to get out of the Hole,' they said. 'All the other fishes saw their chance and escaped when he raised the lid. It was lucky for them he's so big and strong. But the strain of that terrific heave told on him: he sprained a muscle in his tail and it started swelling rather badly. He wanted some quiet place to rest up; and seeing this soft beach handy he crawled in here.'

'Dear me!' said the Doctor. 'I'm terribly sorry. I suppose I should have given some sort of notice that the island was going to be let down. But, to tell the truth, we didn't know it ourselves; it happened by a kind of an accident. Do you imagine the poor fellow is hurt very badly?'

'We're not sure,' said the porpoises, 'because none of us

can speak his language. But we swam right around him on our way in here, and he did not seem to be really seriously injured.'

'Can't any of your people speak shellfish?' the Doctor asked.

'Not a word,' said they. 'It's a most frightfully difficult language.'

'Do you think that you might be able to find me some kind of a fish that could?'

'We don't know,' said the porpoises. 'We might try.'

'I should be extremely grateful to you if you would,' said the Doctor. 'There are many important questions I want to ask this snail – and besides, I would like to do my best to cure his tail for him. It's the least I can do. After all, it was my fault, indirectly, that he got hurt.'

'Well, if you wait here,' said the porpoises, "we'll see what can be done.'

SHELLFISH LANGUAGE AT LAST

MANY and curious were the creatures they produced. First they found a sea-urchin (a funny ball-like little fellow with long whiskers all over him) who said he couldn't speak shellfish but knew starfish language well enough. Then they located a starfish who could speak shellfish moderately well.

Feeling quite encouraged, the Doctor and I, with the porpoises, the urchin, and the starfish swimming alongside, paddled the canoe close to the shell of the Great Snail.

And then began the most curious conversation I have ever witnessed. First the starfish would ask the snail something; and whatever answer the snail gave, the starfish would tell it to the sea-urchin, the urchin would tell it to the porpoises, and the porpoises would tell it to the Doctor.

After this had gone on for some time the Doctor leant over the edge of the canoe and put his face below the water to try to follow the strange conversation more closely.

Hours went by but little by little he found that he was succeeding.

'Stubbins,' he said, lifting his face from the water for the hundredth time, 'I'm beginning to converse directly with the Great Snail. I've managed to convey to him that I think he would be better on a dry part of the beach where I can examine his tail. Will you please go back to town and get my medicine-bag?'

This time when I got back to the shore – with the medicine-bag – I found the snail high and dry on the beach. John Dolittle was examining a swelling on his tail.

From the bag which I had brought, the Doctor took a large bottle of embrocation and began rubbing the sprain. Next he took all the bandages he had in the bag and fastened them end to end. With this he got the sprain strapped to his satisfaction.

The snail really seemed to be quite pleased with the attention he had received; and he stretched himself in lazy comfort when the Doctor was done. In this position, when the shell on his back was empty, you could look right through it and see the palm trees on the other side.

The Doctor seemed very tired. On the way back to the palace Polynesia said: 'Doctor, you ought to take a holiday. All kings take holidays once in a while – every one of them.'

The Doctor made no reply; and we walked on silently towards the town. I could see, nevertheless, that her words had made an impression on him.

After supper he disappeared from the palace without saying where he was going – a thing he had never done before. Of course we all knew where he had gone: back to the beach to sit up with the snail.

When he had gone Polynesia called us together and said: 'Look here, you fellows, we've simply got to get the Doctor to take this holiday somehow – unless we're willing to stay in this blessed island for the rest of our lives.'

'But what difference,' I asked, 'is his taking a holiday going to make?'

Impatiently Polynesia turned to me and said:

'Don't you see? If he has a clear week to get thoroughly

interested in his natural history again – marine stuff, his dream of seeing the floor of the ocean and all that – there may be some chance of his consenting to leave this pesky place. But while he is here on duty as king he never gets a moment to think of anything outside of the business of government.'

'Yes, that's true. He's far too conscientious,' I said.

'And besides,' Polynesia went on, 'his only hope of ever getting away from here would be to leave secretly. Why, I believe if they thought he had any idea of escaping they would put chains on him.'

'Yes, I really think they would,' I agreed. 'Yet without a ship of some kind I don't see how the Doctor is going to get away, even secretly.'

'Well, I'll tell you,' said Polynesia. 'If we do succeed in making him take this holiday, our next step will be to get the sea-snail to promise to take us all in his shell and carry us to the mouth of Puddleby River. If we can once get the snail willing, the temptation will be too much for John Dolittle and he'll come, I know – especially as he'll be able to take those new plants and drugs of Long Arrow's to the English doctors, as well as see the floor of the ocean on the way.'

'How thrilling!' I cried. 'Do you mean the snail could take us under the sea all the way back to Puddleby?'

'Certainly,' said Polynesia, 'a little trip like that is nothing to him. He would crawl along the floor of the ocean and the Doctor could see all the sights. Perfectly simple. Oh, John Dolittle will come all right, if we can only get him to take that holiday – *and* if the snail will consent to give us the ride.'

'Golly, I hope he does!' sighed Jip. 'I'm sick of these beastly tropics – they make you feel so lazy and good-for-nothing. And there are no rats or anything here – not that a fellow would have the energy to chase 'em even if there were. My, wouldn't I be glad to see old Puddleby and the garden again! And won't Dab-Dab be glad to have us back!'

Well, you can guess how glad we were when next morning the Doctor, after his all-night conversation with the snail, told us that he had made up his mind to take the holiday.

'I'm sick of these beastly tropics'

Polynesia was immensely pleased. She at once set quietly to work making arrangements for our departure – taking good care the while that no one should get an inkling of where we were going, what we were taking with us, the hour of our leaving or which of the palace-gates we would go out by.

Long Arrow, who was the only Indian let into the secret of our destination, said he would like to come with us as far as the beach to see the Great Snail; and Polynesia told him to be sure and bring his collection of plants.

Midnight, the hour when most of the townspeople would be

asleep, and the Doctor would be down on the beach sitting up with his patient, she finally chose for our departure.

We had to take a week's food-supply with us for the royal holiday. So, with our other packages, we were heavy laden when on the stroke of twelve we opened the west door of the palace and stepped cautiously and quietly into the moonlit garden. I gently closed the heavy door behind us.

On our arrival at the beach we found the snail already feeling much better and now able to move his tail without pain.

The porpoises (who are by nature inquisitive creatures) were still hanging about in the offing to see if anything of interest was going to happen. Polynesia, the plotter, while the Doctor was occupied with his new patient, signalled to them and drew them aside for a little private chat.

'Now see here, my friends,' said she speaking low, 'you know how much John Dolittle has done for the animals – given his whole life up to them, one might say. Well, here is your chance to do something for him. Listen: if this snail were only willing to take him and us – and a little baggage – not very much, thirty or forty pieces, say – inside his shell and carry us to England, we feel sure that the Doctor would go; because he's just crazy to mess about on the floor of the ocean. Now it is highly important that the Doctor return to his own country to carry on his proper work which means such a lot to the animals of the world. So what we want you to do is to tell the sea-urchin to tell the starfish to tell the snail to take us in his shell and carry us to Puddleby River. Is that plain?'

'Quite, quite,' said the porpoises. 'And we will willingly do our very best to persuade him.'

John Dolittle, unaware of anything save the work he was engaged on, was standing knee-deep in the shallow water, helping the snail try out his mended tail to see if it were well enough to travel on.

Half an hour passed.

What success the porpoises had met with, we did not know, till suddenly the Doctor left the snail's side and came splashing out to us, quite breathless.

'What *do* you think?' he cried. 'While I was talking to the snail just now he offered, of his own accord, to take us all back to England inside his shell. He says he has got to go on a voyage of discovery anyway, to hunt up a new home, now that the Deep Hole is closed. Said it wouldn't be much out of his way to drop us at Puddleby River, if we cared to come along. Goodness, what a chance! I'd love to go. To examine the floor of the ocean all the way from Brazil to Europe! No man ever did it before. What a glorious trip! Oh, that I had never allowed myself to be made king! Now I must see the chance of a lifetime slip by.'

Out of the darkness at my elbow Polynesia rose and quietly moved down to his side.

'Now, Doctor,' said she in a soft persuasive voice as though she were talking to a wayward child, 'you know this king business is not your real work in life. These natives will be able to get along without you. The work you'll do, the information you'll carry home, will be of far more value than what you're doing here.'

'Good friend,' said the Doctor turning to her sadly, 'I cannot leave them now.'

'That's where you're wrong,' Doctor,' said she. 'Now is when you should go. The longer you stay, the harder it will be to leave. Go now. Go tonight.'

'What, steal away without even saying good-bye to them! Why Polynesia, what a thing to suggest!'

'A fat chance they would give you to say good bye!' snorted Polynesia, growing impatient at last. 'I tell you, Doctor, if you go back to that palace tonight, for good-byes or anything else, you will stay there. Now – this moment – is the time for you to go.'

The truth of the old parrot's words seemed to be striking home; for the Doctor stood silent a minute, thinking.

'But there are the notebooks,' he said presently. 'I would have to go back to fetch them.'

'I have them here, Doctor,' said I, speaking up; 'all of them.'

Again he pondered.

'And Long Arrow's collection,' he said. 'I would have to take that also with me.'

'It is here, O Kindly One,' came the Indian's deep voice from the shadow beneath the palm.

'But what about provisions,' asked the Doctor, 'food for the journey?'

'We have a week's supply with us, for our holiday,' said Polynesia; 'that's more than we will need.'

'And then there's my hat,' he said fretfully at last. 'That settles it: 'I'll *have* to go back to the palace. I can't leave without my hat. How could I appear in Puddleby with this crown on my head?'

'Here it is, Doctor,' said I, producing the hat, old, battered, and beloved, from under my coat.

Polynesia had indeed thought of everything.

Yet even now we could see the Doctor was still trying to think up further excuses.

'O Kindly One,' said Long Arrow, 'why tempt ill fortune? Your way is clear. Your future and your work beckon you back to your foreign home beyond the sea. With you will go also what lore I too have gathered for mankind – to lands where it will be of wider use than it can ever be here. I see the glimmerings of dawn in the eastern heaven. Day is at hand. Go before your subjects are abroad. Go before your project is discovered. For truly I believe that if you go not now you will linger the remainder of your days a captive king in Popsipetel.'

Great decisions often take no more than a moment in the making. Against the now paling sky I saw the Doctor's figure suddenly stiffen. Slowly he lifted the Sacred Crown from his head and laid it on the sands. And when he spoke his voice was choked with tears.

'They will find it here,' he murmured, 'when they come to search for me. And they will know that I have gone ... My children, my poor children! – I wonder will they ever understand why it was I left them ... I wonder will they ever understand – and forgive.'

He took his old hat from me; then facing Long Arrow, gripped his outstretched hand in silence.

'You decide aright, O Kindly One,' said the Indian, 'though

He laid it on the sands

none will miss and mourn you more than Long Arrow, the son of Golden Arrow. Farewell, and may good fortune ever lead you by the hand!'

It was the first and only time I ever saw the Doctor weep. Without a word to any of us, he turned and moved down the beach into the shallow water of the sea.

The snail humped up its back and made an opening between its shoulders and the edge of its shell. The Doctor clambered up and passed within. We followed him, after handing up the baggage. The opening shut tight with a whistling suction noise.

Then turning in the direction of the east, the great creature began moving smoothly forward, down the slope into the deeper waters.

Just as the swirling dark green surf was closing in above our heads, the big morning sun popped his rim up over the edge of the ocean. And through our transparent walls of pearl we saw the watery world about us suddenly light up with that most wondrously colourful of visions, a daybreak beneath the sea.

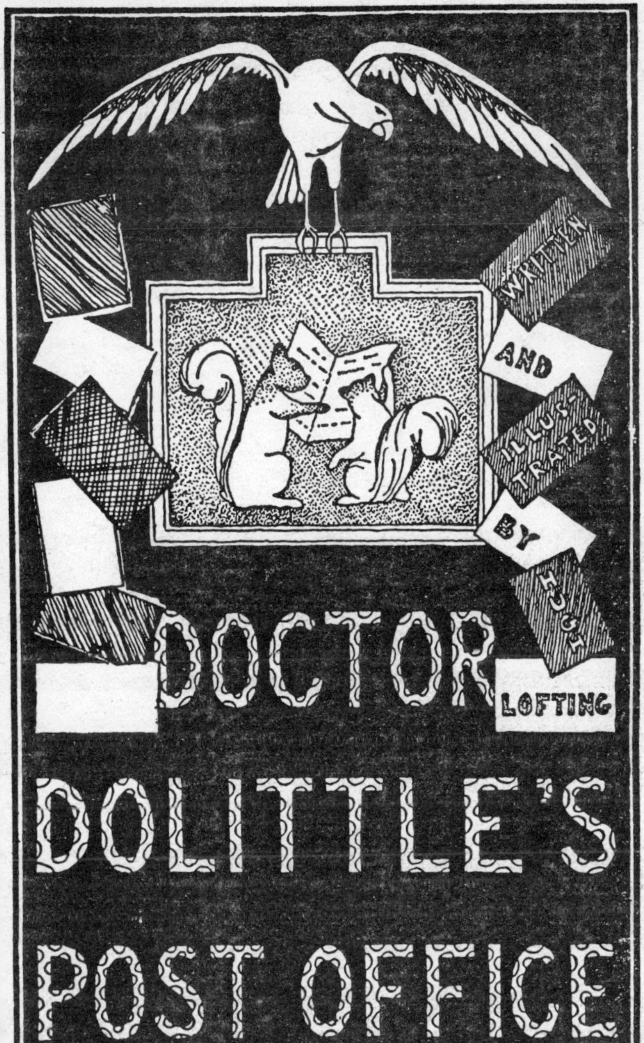
WRITTEN
AND
ILLUS-
TRATED
BY
HUGH
LOFTING
DOCTOR
DOLITTLE'S
POST OFFICE

THE HOLIDAY

NEARLY all of the history of Doctor Dolittle's Post Office took place when he was returning from a voyage to West Africa.

The trip had begun with a timid question from the pushmi-pullyu: 'I'm a little homesick, sir. Would you mind if I returned to Africa for a few weeks – just to wander about my old grazing grounds for a while?'

'Why, no,' said the Doctor. 'I think it could be arranged.'

With that all the Doctor's animal friends spoke up at once.

'Can I go?' squeaked Gub-Gub.

'I need a holiday too,' said Jip.

'You're not going to leave me at home, are you, Doctor?' asked Dab-Dab.

'What about me?' squeaked Whitey.

'Wait a minute!' interrupted the Doctor. 'I haven't said anyone except the pushmi-pullyu was going.'

'Why don't we all go?' asked Too-Too. 'There's plenty of money for a few weeks' holiday.'

'Well, Too-Too,' said the Doctor, 'that sounds most inviting. It is pretty chilly here in England.'

No one could make up his mind quicker than the Doctor when a voyage was in prospect.

He bought a little sailing-boat – very old and battered and worn, but a good sound craft for any kind of weather. Provisions were put aboard for all the animals and they sailed down the south coast of the Bight of Benin.

After visiting many African kingdoms and the strange tribes, they stopped off at a small coastal country called Fantippo. This kingdom had a rather peculiar post office. For one thing, it was, of course, quite unusual to find a post office or regular mails of any kind in an African kingdom in those days.

When Doctor Dolittle arrived he found it in pretty bad shape. He saw that it worked well enough for local mails – but even that was slow. Letters took as long as a week to be delivered a few miles. You see, there was no regular route and the postmen often went fishing instead of delivering the mails.

So the Doctor invited the King of Fantippo to tea one day and explained how the mails were handled in other countries of the world. The King listened attentively and then asked the Doctor to come ashore and arrange the post office for him and put it in order so it would work properly.

After some persuasion the Doctor consented to this proposal, feeling that perhaps he could do some good. Little did he realize what great labours he was taking upon himself.

He found the post office in a terrible state. There were letters everywhere – on the floors, in old drawers, knocking about on desks, even lying on the pavement outside the post office door.

It took weeks and weeks of terrific labour before the Doctor finally got the Domestic Mails in pretty good shape. But the Foreign Mails were a harder problem because mail ships did not stop often at Fantippo.

One day, very early in the morning, when the Doctor was lying in bed, wondering what he could do about straightening out the Foreign Mail service, Dab-Dab and Jip brought him in his breakfast on a tray and told him they had something they would like to talk about.

'But not right now, Doctor,' said Dab-Dab. 'You have your breakfast first.'

'No, no!' replied the Doctor. 'You stay and talk. I'll have my breakfast meanwhile, if you don't mind.' He cracked off the top of a hardboiled egg. 'What can I do for you?'

Dab-Dab was the first to speak. 'Why don't you get the birds to help you deliver the Foreign Mails?' she asked.

'They can fly all over the world,' added Jip.

'Good gracious!' cried the Doctor, swallowing a piece of toast.

'What a splendid idea! I hadn't thought about that. Thank you, Dab-Dab and Jip. I'll get on to it right away.'

He brushed the toast crumbs off the bedclothes, handed the tray to Dab-Dab and rushed off to dress.

'Jip!' he called from the bathroom. 'Send for Speedy-the-Skimmer. I'll need to talk to him about this, and come along with us when you find him. I'll meet you under the palms where it's cool.'

As Dab-Dab was leaving the room the Doctor stuck his head out of the bathroom doorway. He had lathered his face and was shaving.

'You come too, Dab-Dab,' he said, sounding kind of foamy.

'Oh, no, Doctor,' replied Dab-Dab. 'I'm much too busy. This room needs cleaning from top to bottom. You and Jip can manage without me.'

And she left carrying the Doctor's breakfast tray in one claw as she hopped down the corridor to the kitchen.

When Jip returned with Speedy, the Doctor was waiting under the palm trees. They sat down in the shade and for the first time plans for the great service which was to be known as the Swallow Mail were discussed.

'Now, my idea, Speedy, is this,' said the Doctor. 'Regular foreign mails are difficult because so few boats ever call here for mail. Now, how would it be if the swallows did the letter carrying?'

'Well,' said Speedy. 'That would be possible. But, of course, we could only do it during certain months of the year we were in Africa. And then we could only take letters to the mild and warm countries. We should get frozen if we had to carry mail where severe winters were going on.'

'Oh, of course,' said the Doctor. 'I wouldn't expect you to do that. But I had thought we might get the other birds to help – cold-climate birds, hot-climate ones and temperate. And if some of the trips were too far or disagreeable for one kind of birds to make, we could deliver the mail in relays. I mean, for instance, a letter going from here to the North Pole could be carried by the swallows as far as the north end of Africa. From there it

The houseboat post office off the shores of Fantippo

would be taken by the thrushes up to the top of Scotland. There the seagulls would take it from the thrushes and carry it as far as Greenland. And from there penguins would take it to the North Pole. What do you think?'

'I think it is a wonderful idea!' said Speedy.

Well, with the help of Speedy the new Foreign Mail Service was established. The King of Fantippo had his builders construct a beautiful houseboat to be anchored off a near-by island and which was the headquarters for all the Foreign Mail services. Here the birds could pick up the mail and begin their relay delivery of letters and packages to all countries of the world.

Then Dab-Dab, Jip, Too-Too, Gub-Gub, the pushmi-pullyu and the white mouse were brought from the Doctor's ship and the Doctor and his family settled down to live at the Foreign Mail post office for the remainder of their stay.

THE BIRDS THAT HELPED COLUMBUS

AFTER the Doctor had written his first letter by Swallow Mail to the Cat's-meat-Man he began to think of all the other people to whom he had neglected to write for years and years. And very soon every spare moment he had was filled in writing to friends and acquaintances everywhere.

And he sent letters to various fellow naturalists whom he knew in different countries and gave them a whole lot of information about the yearly flights or migrations of birds. Because, of course, in the bird-mail business he learned a great deal on that subject that had never been known to naturalists before.

Outside the post office he had a notice board set up on which were posted the Outgoing and Incoming Mails. The notices would read something like this:

Next Wednesday, July 18th, the Red-Winged Plovers will leave this office for Denmark and points on the Skager Rack. Post your mail early, please. All letters should bear a fourpenny stamp. Small packages will also be carried on this flight for Morocco, Portugal, and the Channel Islands.

Whenever a new flight of birds was expected at the island the Doctor always had a big supply of food of their particular kind got ready for their arrival beforehand. He had at the big meeting with the leaders put down in his notebook the dates of all the yearly flights of the different kinds of birds, where they started from and where they went to. And this notebook was kept with great care.

One day Speedy was sitting on top of the weighing scales

while the Doctor was sorting a large pile of outgoing letters. Suddenly the Skimmer cried out:

'Great heavens, Doctor, I've gained an ounce! I'll never be able to fly in the races again. Look, it says four and a half ounces!'

'No, Speedy,' said the Doctor. 'See, you have an ounce weight on the pan as well as yourself. That makes you only three and a half ounces.'

'Oh,' said the Skimmer, 'is that the trouble? I was never good at arithmetic. What a relief! Thank goodness, I haven't gained!'

'Listen, Speedy,' said the Doctor, 'in this batch of mail we have a lot of letters for Panama. What mails have we got going out tomorrow?'

'I'm not sure,' said Speedy. 'I'll go and look at the noticeboard. I think it's the Golden Jays . . . Yes,' he said, coming back in a moment, 'that's right, the Golden Jays tomorrow, Tuesday, the 15th, weather permitting.'

'Where are they bound for, Speedy?' asked the Doctor. 'My notebook's in the safe.'

'From Dahomey to Venezuela,' said Speedy, raising his right foot to smother a yawn.

'Good,' said John Dolittle. 'Then they can take these Panama letters for me. It won't be much out of their way. What do Golden Jays eat?'

'They are very fond of acorns,' said Speedy.

'All right,' said the Doctor. 'Please tell Gub-Gub for me to go across to the island and get the wild boars to gather up a couple of sacks of acorns. I want all the birds who work for us to have a good feed before they leave the Main Office for their flights.'

The next morning when the Doctor woke up he heard a tremendous chattering all around the post office and he knew that the Golden Jays had arrived overnight. And after he had dressed and come out on to the veranda, there, sure enough, they were – myriads of very handsome gold-and-black birds, swarming everywhere, gossiping away at a great rate and gobbling up the acorns laid out for them in bushels.

'Great heavens, Doctor, I've gained an ounce!'

The leader, who already knew the Doctor, of course, came forward to get orders and to see how much mail there was to be carried.

After everything had been arranged and the leader had decided he need expect no tornadoes or bad weather for the next twenty-four hours, he gave a command. Then all the birds rose in the air to fly away – whistling farewell to Postmaster General Dolittle and the Head Office.

'Oh, by the way, Doctor,' said the leader, turning back a moment, 'did you ever hear of a man called Christopher Columbus?'

'Oh, surely,' said the Doctor. 'He discovered America in 1492.'

'Well, I just wanted to tell you,' said the Jay, 'that if it hadn't been for an ancestor of mine he wouldn't have discovered it in 1492 – later perhaps, but not in 1492.'

'Oh, indeed!' said John Dolittle. 'Tell me more about it.' And he pulled a notebook out of his pocket and started to write.

'Well,' said the Jay, 'the story was handed down to me by my mother, who heard it from my grandmother, who got it from my great-grandmother, and so on, way back to an ancestor of ours who lived in America in the fifteenth century. Our kind of birds in those days did not come across to this side of the Atlantic, neither summer nor winter. We used to spend from March to September in the Bermudas and the rest of the year in Venezuela. And when we made the autumn journey south we used to stop at the Bahama Islands to rest on the way.

'The autumn of the year 1492 was a stormy season. Gales and squalls were blowing up all the time, and we did not get started on our trip until the second week in October. My ancestor had been the leader of the flock for a long time. But he had grown sort of old and feeble and a younger bird was elected in his place to lead the Golden Jays to Venezuela that year. The new leader was a conceited youngster, and because he had been chosen he thought he knew everything about navigation and weather and sea crossings.

'Shortly after the birds started they sighted, to their great astonishment, a number of boats sailing on a westward course. This was about halfway between the Bermudas and the Bahamas. The ships were much larger than anything they had ever seen before. All they had been accustomed to up to that time were little canoes, with Indians in them.

'The new leader immediately got scared and gave the order for the Jays to swing in farther towards the land, so they wouldn't be seen by the men who crowded these large boats. He was a superstitious leader and anything he didn't understand he kept away from. But my ancestor did not go with the flock, but made straight for the ships.

'He was gone about twenty minutes, and presently he flew

'The sailors were ready to kill their admiral'

after the other birds and said to the new leader: "Over there in those ships a brave man is in great danger. They come from Europe, seeking land. The sailors, not knowing how near they are to sighting it, have mutinied against their admiral. I am an old bird and I know this brave seafarer. Once when I was making a crossing – the first I ever made – a gale came up and I was separated from my fellows. For three days I had to fly with the battering wind. And finally I was blown eastward near the Old World. Just when I was ready to drop into the sea from exhaustion I spied a ship. I simply had to rest. I was weather-beaten and starving. So I made for the boat and fell half dead upon the deck. The sailors were going to put me in a cage. But the captain of the ship – this same navigator whose life is now threatened by his rebellious crew in those ships over there – fed me crumbs and nursed me back to life. Then he let me go free, to fly to Venezuela when the weather was fair. We are land birds. Let us now save this good man's life by going to his ship and showing ourselves to his sailors. They will then know that land is near and be obedient to their captain." '

'Yes, yes,' said the Doctor. 'Go on. I remember Columbus writing of land birds in his diary. Go on.'

'So,' said the Jay, 'the whole flock turned and made for Columbus's fleet. They were only just in time. For sailors were ready to kill their admiral, who, they said, had brought them on a fool's errand to find land where there was none. He must turn back and sail for Spain, they said, or be killed.

'But when the sailors saw a great flock of land birds passing over the ship going south-west instead of west, they took new heart, for they were sure land must lie not far to the south-westward.

'So we led them on to the Bahamas. And on the seventh day, very early in the morning, the crew, with a cry of "Land! Land!" fell down upon their knees and gave thanks to heaven. Watling's Island, one of the smaller Bahamas, lay ahead of them smiling in the sea.

'Then the sailors gathered about the admiral, Christopher Columbus, whom a little before they were going to kill, and cheered and called him the greatest navigator in the world – which, in truth, he was. But even Columbus himself never learned to his dying day that it was the weather-beaten bird who had fallen on his friendly deck some years before who had led him by the shortest cut to the land of the New World.

'So you see, Doctor,' the Jay ended, picking up his letters and getting ready to fly, 'if it hadn't been for my ancestor, Christopher Columbus would have had to turn back to please his sailors, or be killed. If it hadn't been for him America would not have been discovered in 1492 – later, perhaps, but not in 1492. Good-bye! I must be going. Thanks for the acorns.'

DOCTOR DOLITTLE'S

CARAVAN

WRITTEN AND ILLUSTRATED BY

HUGH LOFTING

THE DOLITTLE CIRCUS STAFF HOLDS A MEETING

THE Canary Opera's run at the Regent's Theatre broke all records in successful theatrical productions. Week after week went by and instead of the attendance falling off, the house seemed packed a little tighter – and the crowd turned away a little bigger – every night.

The One Hundredth Performance was celebrated with another dinner at Patti's in the Strand – the first banquet was before the opening night. But on this occasion some of the faces that surrounded the table at the first celebration were absent. The reason for this was that many of the original staff of the Dolittle Circus had made enough money to retire.

When the meal was over and speeches came to be made, Hop the clown rose and told the company that this was his farewell appearance in public. He too, he said, had made enough money to retire and much as he disliked the idea of parting from his excellent friend and manager, John Dolittle (cries of 'Hear! Hear!'), he had waited all his life to travel abroad. And now at last he had the means to do it. His dog Swizzle, however, had chosen to remain with the Doctor, so that he did not feel he was altogether deserting the show, since his dog, the companion of many years of circus life, would remain in the ring to keep his memory green.

At this dinner the dress of the company was noticeably different from that worn at the first. Mrs Mugg, the Mistress of the Wardrobe and chronicler of the Dolittle Circus, fairly shimmered with jewellery. Matthew, too, when he arose and launched into a long and eloquent speech, was seen to be wearing three enormous diamonds in the bosom of his shirt and another, even larger, in a ring upon his finger. The Doctor himself wore a brand new dress-suit made by a Bond Street tailor; but he said it did not feel nearly as comfortable as the one that had split up the back at the dinner given to welcome his operatic company to London.

The Doctor, in his own address, said he was glad that his remaining so long in the show business had given opportunities for many to realize their ambitions and to do those things they wanted most to do.

They had now been in London three months, and the budding of spring on the park trees reminded him of his own home in Puddleby, of his garden and his plants which he had so long neglected. Before another three months had passed, he said, he hoped that he himself would be able to retire from the theatrical world, and that the other members of the company who made Canary Opera the success it was would be sufficiently well off to do likewise, if they wished.

The departure of Hop the clown from the Dolittle Circus was an event of importance. Both Swizzle and he wept on one another's necks when they came to say good-bye. And it was only after Hop had promised, through the Doctor, that he would keep him posted by letter on how he got on, that the circus dog was consoled. Even then all that night he kept Jip and Toby awake, having qualms and scruples about deserting his old master.

'You know,' he'd say suddenly when the others were just feeling sure and glad that he'd gone to sleep, 'it isn't as if I *had* to let him go alone. They say a dog's place is by his master's side. He was always an awfully kind, considerate sort of boss, was Hop. I feel a terrible pig deserting him after all these years.'

'Oh, forget about it and go to sleep!' said Toby irritably. 'I don't see what you're blaming yourself for. You worked for your living. You helped his act in the ring – in fact, you were the better clown of the two. The audiences always laughed more at your antics than they did at his. Now he's going out of the show business with plenty of money – which you helped him make. If you prefer to stay with Doctor Dolittle while Hop travels round the world enjoying himself that's your business.'

'Yes, I suppose so,' said Swizzle thoughtfully. 'Still, he was such a decent fellow, was Hop.'

'And so was Henry Crockett, *my* man,' said Toby. 'But I left him, or rather he left me, in the same way. I wanted to stay with the Doctor, too. I helped him make the Punch-and-Judy show a success. I don't feel guilty. My goodness! After all, our lives are our own even if we are dogs.'

As it happened, the Doctor himself was wakeful, too, that night, thinking over various problems connected with the opera; and as the dogs' quarters were situated in the passage outside his room he had heard the whole conversation.

What Toby (who, as you will remember, always insisted upon his rights) had said about their lives being their own, even if they were dogs, set John Dolittle thinking. And the next day, after he had spent more than an hour talking over money matters with Too-Too the accountant, he called a meeting of the circus staff.

In one of the larger sideshow tents where they were all collected, Manager Dolittle rose and made an address, first in English to the people and then in animal-language to the rest.

'The cooperative system,' he said, 'which we have followed has proved, I think I can say, a great success. But I feel that it is only fair that now when we have a big balance in the bank, due largely to the Canary Opera's reception, the animals who have taken so important a part in all our shows should share in the profits. And in any case it is desirable that all our performers should be provided for when we disband. I therefore propose that the animal members of the staff share with the rest of us on the same basis and that bank accounts should be opened in their own names.'

Then followed a short discussion. Of course, the animals were all in favour of the Doctor's idea, with one or two exceptions; and the only active objections came from a tent-rigger and the clerk who sold the tickets at the circus box office. They said they couldn't see what animals wanted money for, and they opposed the idea.

Talking over money matters with Too-Too

However, the other three human members present – the Doctor, Matthew and Fred the animals' caretaker – were in favour, and the motion was carried, on the human side, three votes to two.

In talking over this matter that same night at their after-the-show supper in the town house, the Doctor further explained his reasons for proposing such an idea.

'You see,' said he, pouring himself out a second cup of cocoa, 'I am not only thinking of providing for the animals in their old age, when perhaps I shall no longer be here for them to come to.

But I hope by this to improve the standing of animals in general. There is an old saying, "Money talks," and – '

' "Monkey talks," did you say?' asked Gub-Gub.

'No. *Money* talks,' the Doctor repeated. 'It is a horrible thing, money. But it is also horrible to be the only one who hasn't got any. One of my chief complaints against people has always been that they had no respect for animals. But many people have a great respect for money. Animals with bank accounts of their own will be in a position to insist upon respect.'

'But how about their making out cheques, Doctor?' asked Too-Too the accountant.

'I have already gone into that matter,' said John Dolittle, 'with lawyers and several bank managers. Most of them thought I was crazy and wouldn't listen to me at all. But two banks, the Eastminster and Chelsea, and the Middlesex Joint Stock Bank, agreed that if some person were given what is called power of attorney – and did all the writing of the cheques, the depositing and the drawing – those banks would have no objection to putting accounts in their books under the names of animals.'

Gub-Gub, when he was handed a cheque-book of his own, was highly delighted. He used to bother Too-Too four and five times a day to know how much money he had in the Eastminster and Chelsea. And he boasted to every pig he met that they had better be careful how they talked to him or he would hire a lawyer and have him hauled into court.

Jip had an account opened at the Middlesex Joint Stock Bank – and a very substantial balance he had when the Doctor had placed the money from Monsieur Poulain to the dog's credit. You may remember, Jip was hired as an expert on smells to assist the perfumer in developing new and tantalizing odours for ladies of fashion.

Dab Dab said she had no preference where she banked. All she wanted to do was to keep part of the money safe from the Doctor's spending – to be used later, if need be, to get him back to Puddleby and a peaceful life.

WAYS OF SPENDING MONEY

It was the Doctor's intention, once he had banked the money in the animals' names, to allow them to do what they liked with it, to give them complete control. To tell the truth, he was vastly interested to see what they would do with it. It was a new experiment and although the Doctor did not influence them at all in the matter, they did influence one another quite a good deal.

On the evening of the day when they first came into their fortunes the Doctor was kept late at the theatre talking with the managers; and the animal household sat down to supper in the kitchen of the town house without him.

'What are you going to do with *your* money, Jip?' asked the white mouse.

'I'm not quite sure yet,' said Jip. 'I've often had a notion that I'd like to set up a dog's soup kitchen in the East End – a sort of free hotel for dogs. You've no idea what a lot of them are starving around the streets. A place where the waifs and strays could come and get a bone or a square meal and perhaps a bed for the night – and no questions asked – would be a good thing. I spoke of it once to the Doctor, and he said he would see what could be done about it.'

'Oh, no, you don't!' snapped Dab-Dab. 'No more homes for broken-down horses or stray dogs, thank you! I know what that means. You remember the Retired Cab-Horses' Association? That's the very thing we want to keep the Doctor away from. I'm going to leave my money where it is, in the bank. John Dolittle may be rich now – if what Too-Too says is true, he's as rich as the Lord Mayor of London – but nobody can get through money the way he can once he gets started. The day will come when he's poor again, never fear. Then, if we've still got the money that he put in the bank for us, we'll be able to help him. He can say all he likes about our having earned it. But you know very well if it wasn't for him we wouldn't have a penny.'

The animal household sat down to supper

'With my money,' said Gub-Gub, blowing out his chest, 'I'm going to set myself up in a business as a greengrocer.'

'Oh, for heaven's sake, listen to that!' groaned Dab-Dab, rolling her eyes.

'Well, why not?' said Gub-Gub. I'm rich enough now to buy all the cabbages in England. I'm one of the wealthiest animals in London.'

'You're the stupidest pig in the world,' snorted the housekeeper. 'And you'd probably eat all your vegetables instead of selling them. If you must go into the greengrocery business, for

Gub-Gub gets his trotters polished

pity's sake wait till we've got the family back to Puddleby.'

And so, in spite of the fact that they were the first animals to obtain the independence that comes with money, in the end, after they had talked things over among themselves, they did not show any disposition towards reckless or foolish spending.

But of course it would be unnatural to expect that the animals would not wish to buy something with their new wealth. And each in his own way (after he had questioned Too-Too about his balance) did a little shopping – just to celebrate, as Gub-Gub put it.

The white mouse's first purchase was a selection of foreign cheeses. He went with the Doctor to a very expensive West End grocery and bought a quarter of a pound of every kind of cheese that had ever been invented.

Gub-Gub's own investment was a selection of hot-house vegetables and fruits. He bought some of everything that was out of season, from artichokes to grapes. A lady customer who happened to be in the shop was very shocked at the idea of these delicacies being bought for a pig (Gub-Gub sampled most of them right away). And being a busybody, she remonstrated with the Doctor for giving such dainties to him.

'Tell her I've bought them with my own money,' said Gub-Gub, sauntering out on to the street with his nose in the air and his mouth full of asparagus.

Another of Gub-Gub's new luxuries was having his trotters shined every day. An arrangement was made with a shoeblack, a small boy who lived not very far from the Doctor's town house. And every morning Gub-Gub stood very elegantly on the steps while his hoofs were polished till he could see his face in them. Dab-Dab was furious at this. She called it a vain, nonsensical waste of money. But the Doctor said it was not a very extravagant matter (it only cost a penny a day); and, after all, what was the use of Gub-Gub's having money of his own if he wasn't allowed to spend at least a little of it on frivolities?

'But why should he?' said Dab-Dab, her feathers bristling with indignation. 'It doesn't do him any good to have his silly feet polished, and it certainly doesn't do us any good.'

'What an idea!' said Gub-Gub. 'Why I'm the best dressed pig in Town.'

'Best *dressed*,' snorted Dab-Dab, 'when you don't wear any clothes!'

'Well, I'm the best groomed anyhow,' said Gub-Gub. 'And it's right that I should be. I have my reputation to keep up. Everywhere I go children point at me and say, "Look, there's Gub-Gub, the famous comedian!" '

'The famous nincompoop, more likely,' muttered Dab-Dab, turning back to her cooking. 'I suppose I can work myself to death over the kitchen sink while that overfed booby goes mincing round the streets, cutting a dash.'

'Well, but, Dab-Dab,' said the Doctor, 'you don't *have* to do the housekeeping, you know – not now any more – if you would sooner not. We can afford to engage a woman housekeeper or a butler.'

'No,' said Dab-Dab, 'I'm not complaining about that. Nobody else could take care of you the way I can. This is my job. I wouldn't want to let anyone else take it over. The thing I object to is that stupid pig standing on the front steps every morning so the people passing on the street will see him having his shoes shined. He doesn't really enjoy being clean. He just thinks it's smart.'

But some of the animals' first use of money was not that of buying in shops. Dab-Dab finally decided that she *would* hire a scullery-maid to help her with the washing up. The housekeeper insisted that the new servant's wages should be paid for out of her bank account and not the Doctor's.

'After all, she is my assistant, and I ought to pay her,' said she. 'The Doctor's money will be needed for enough things without a scullery-maid's wages. Of course, she'll have to sleep out; I haven't room for her in the house unless I put her in with the pelicans. And they might object to that – a scullery-maid – as soon as animals go on the stage they start putting on airs. Well, as the Doctor says, we shall see.'

The scullery-maid was engaged, and after she had been instructed in her duties by Housekeeper Dab-Dab (the Doctor acting as interpreter, of course) she fitted into the strange household extremely well.

Swizzle's first use of his bank account was rather peculiar and opened up still another new possibility for moneyed animals. He discovered, while in the city (through some of the sick dogs who visited the Doctor's surgery on Greenheath), that he had a sister living in a suburb on the south bank of the Thames. Swizzle went to visit her when he learned of her whereabouts and took the Doctor along for a walk. He found that his sister had been married (it was seven years since he had seen her last) and now had a family of five very jolly little puppies. Two of them, however, were somewhat ailing, and Swizzle's sister (her name was Maggie) was very glad that the Doctor had accompanied her brother on the visit because she could now get the benefit of his professional advice.

'Well,' said John Dolittle, 'there's nothing seriously wrong with any of your children, Maggie. What they need is fresh air, all of them. London air isn't much to boast of at best. But, you see, this shed here where you have your kennel is very close and airless. You must get the puppies out more.'

'But how can I, Doctor?' said Maggie. 'They're scarcely able to walk yet. And even if they were, I'd never dare to take them on the streets till they have more sense – for fear they'd get run over.'

'Humph!' said John Dolittle thoughtfully, 'Yes, that's so.'

'I tell you what, Doctor,' said Swizzle suddenly. 'Let's hire a nursemaid for my sister's family. Now I've got money of my own I can pay for one.'

And that was what was finally done. A day or so later the citizens of London were provided with still another Dolittle surprise. A smart nursemaid was seen walking through the streets pushing a perambulator with five puppies in it, each wearing a warm knitted coat of white wool. Sometimes they were accompanied by their proud uncle, Swizzle, the clown dog from the Dolittle Circus.

The nursemaid was discharged, however, after her second week of employment and another engaged in her place. The puppies had complained that she would clean their ears in public, and they demanded a nursemaid who would be more considerate of their dignity.

DOCTOR DOLITTLE

AND THE GREEN CANARY

WRITTEN AND ILLUSTRATED BY
HUGH LOFTING

THE DOCTOR BUYS THE GREEN CANARY

THIS is the story of how the Doctor came to buy Pippinella, the green canary. It happened during the time the Dolittle Circus had its headquarters on Greenheath just outside London.

One evening the Doctor went for a walk with Matthew Mugg and Jip. They had been busy all day with the crowds that came to see the circus and needed greatly to get away from all the confusion.

After going through the main streets, they came to an inn which had tables and chairs set outside before the door. It was a warm evening and the Doctor and Matthew sat down at the inn table to drink a glass of ale.

While they were resting and watching the quiet life of the town the song of a bird reached their ears. It was extraordinarily beautiful, at times tremendously powerful, at others soft and low and mysterious – but always changing. The singer, whoever he was, never repeated himself.

The Doctor had written books on bird-songs and he was interested.

'Do you hear that, Matthew?' he asked.

'Great, ain't it?' said the Cat's-meat-Man. 'Must be a nightingale – up on them big elms by the church there.'

'No,' said the Doctor, 'that's no nightingale. That's a canary. He is singing scraps of a nightingale's song which he has picked up – and parts of many others, too. But he has a canary's voice, for all that. Listen; now he's imitating a thrush.'

They sat a while longer and the bird ran through a wonderful range of imitations.

'You know, Matthew,' said the Doctor, 'I think I'd like to have a canary in the wagon. They're awfully good company.

I've never bought one, because I hate to see birds in cages. But with those who are born in captivity I suppose it's really all right. Let's go down the street and see if we can get a glimpse of this songster.'

So after the Doctor had paid for the ale they left the tables and walked along towards the church. But before they reached it they saw there were several shops to pass. Presently the Doctor stopped.

'Look, Matthew,' said he. 'One of those shops is an animal shop. That's where the canary is. I hate animal shops – the poor creatures usually look so neglected. The proprietors always keep too many – more than they can look after properly. And they usually smell so stuffy and close – the shops, I mean. I never go into them now. I don't even pass one if I can help it.'

'Why?' asked Matthew.

'Well,' said the Doctor, 'ever since I became sort of known among the animals the poor beasts all talk to me as soon as I go in, begging me to buy them – birds and rabbits and guinea pigs and everything. I think I'll turn back and go around another way, so I won't have to pass the window.'

But just as the Doctor was about to return towards the inn the beautiful voice of the song-bird burst out again and he hesitated.

'He's marvellous,' said John Dolittle, 'simply superb!'

'Why not hurry by with just one eye open?' said Matthew. 'Maybe you could spot the bird without stopping.'

'All right,' said the Doctor. And putting on a brisk pace, he strode towards the shop. In passing it he just gave one glance in at the window and hurried on.

'Well,' asked Matthew, as the Doctor paused on the other side, 'did you see which bird it was?'

'Yes,' said John Dolittle. 'It's that green canary near the door, the one in the small wooden cage, marked three shillings. Listen, Matthew, go in and buy him for me. I can afford that much, I think. I dare not go myself. Everything in the place will clamour at me at once. I have an idea those white rabbits recognized me already. You go for me ... Don't forget – the green canary in the wooden cage near the door, marked three shillings. Here's the money.'

So Matthew Mugg went into the store with the three shillings, while the Doctor waited outside the window of the shop next door.

The Cat's-meat-Man wasn't gone very long – and when he returned he had no canary with him.

'You made a mistake, Doctor,' said he. 'The bird you spoke of is a hen and they don't sing. The one we heard is a bright yellow cock, right outside the shop. They want two pounds ten for him. He's a prize bird, they say, and the best singer they ever had.'

'How extraordinary!' said the Doctor. 'Are you sure?'

And, forgetting for the moment all about his intention of not being seen by the animals in the shop, he moved up to the window and pointed again to the green canary.

'That's the bird I meant,' he said. 'Did you ask about that one? – Oh, Lord! Now I've done it. She has recognized me.'

The green canary near the door-end of the window, seeing the famous Doctor pointing to her, evidently expected him to buy her. She was already making signs to him through the glass and jumping about her cage with joy.

The Doctor, quite unable to afford two pounds ten for the other bird, was beginning to move away. But the expression in the little green canary's face as she realized he didn't mean to buy her after all was pitiful to see.

John Dolittle had not walked with Matthew more than a hundred yards down the street before he stopped again.

'It's no use,' said he. 'I'll have to buy her, I suppose – even if she can't sing. That's always the way if I go near an animal shop. I always have to buy the wretchedest and most useless thing they have there. Go back and get her.'

Once more the Cat's-meat-Man went into the shop and presently returned with a small cage covered over with brown paper.

'We must hurry, Matthew,' said the Doctor. 'It's nearly time that the tea was served and Theodosia always finds it hard to attend to it without our help.'

On reaching the circus the Doctor was immediately called away on important business connected with the show. He asked Matthew to take the canary to the wagon, and he was himself occupied with one thing and another until supper-time.

And even when he finally returned to his wagon his mind was so taken up with the things of the day that he had forgotten for the moment all about the canary he had bought. He sank wearily into a chair as he entered and Too-Too, the accountant, immediately engaged him in a financial conversation.

But the dull discussion of money and figures had hardly begun before the Doctor's attention was distracted by a very agreeable sound. It was the voice of a bird warbling ever so softly.

'Great heavens!' the Doctor whispered. 'Where's that coming from?'

The sound grew and grew – the most beautiful singing that John Dolittle had ever heard, even superior to that which he had listened to outside the inn. To ordinary ears it would have been wonderful enough, but to the Doctor, who understood canary-language and could follow the words of the song being sung, it was an experience to be remembered.

It was a long poem, telling of many things – of many lands and many loves, of little adventures and great adventures, and the melody, now sad, now gay – fierce, now soft, was more wonderful than the finest nightingale singing at his best.

'Where is it coming from?' the Doctor repeated, completely mystified.

'From that covered cage up on the shelf,' said Too-Too.

'Great heavens!' the Doctor cried. 'The bird I bought this afternoon.'

He sprang up and tore the wrapping paper aside. The song ceased. The little green canary peered out at him through the torn hole.

'I thought you were a hen,' said the Doctor.

'So I am,' said the bird.

'But you sing!'

'Well, why not?'

She laughed a long trilling laugh

'But hen canaries don't sing.'

The little green bird laughed a long, trilling, condescending sort of laugh.

'That old story – it's so amusing!' she said. 'It was invented by the cocks, you know – the conceited males. The hens have by far the better voices. But the cocks don't like us to sing. They peck us if we do. Some years ago a movement was started – "Singing for Women", it was called. Some of us hens got together to assert our rights. But there were an awful lot of old-fashioned ones – old maids, you know – who still thought it was unmaidenly to sing. They said that a hen's place was on the nest – that singing was for men only. So the movement failed. That's why people still believe that hens *can't* sing.'

'But you didn't sing in the shop?' said the Doctor.

'Neither would you – in *that* shop,' said the canary. 'The smell of the place was enough to choke you.'

'Well, why did you sing now?'

'Because I realized, after the man you sent came in a second time, that you had wanted to buy that stupid yellow cock who had been bawling out of tune all afternoon. I knew, of course, that you only sent the man back to get me out of kindness. So I thought I'd like to repay you by showing you what we women can do in the musical line.'

'Marvellous!' said the Doctor. 'You certainly make that other fellow sound like a second-rate singer. You are a contralto, I see.'

'A mezzo-contralto,' the canary corrected. 'But I can go right up through the highest soprano range when I want to.'

'What is your name?' asked the Doctor.

'Pippinella,' the bird replied.

'What was that you were singing just now?'

'I was singing you the story of my life.'

'But it was in verse.'

'Yes, I made it into poetry – just to amuse myself. We cage birds have a lot of spare time on our hands, when there are no eggs to sit on or young ones to feed.'

'Humph!' said the Doctor. 'You are a great artist – a poet and singer.'

'And a musician!' said the canary quietly. 'The composition is entirely my own. You noticed I used none of the ordinary bird-songs – except the love song of the greenfinch at the part where I am telling of my faithless husband running off to America and leaving me weeping by the shore.'

Dab-Dab at this moment came in to announce that supper was ready, but to Gub-Gub's disgust the Doctor brushed everything aside in the excitement of a new interest. Diving into an old portfolio, he brought out a blank musical manuscript book in which he sometimes wrote down pieces for the flute, his own favourite instrument.

'Excuse me,' he said to the canary, 'but would you mind starting the story of your life all over again. It interests me immensely.'

'Certainly,' said the little bird. 'Have my drinking trough filled with water, will you please? It got emptied with the shaking coming here. I like to moisten my throat occasionally when I am singing long songs.'

'Of course, of course!' said the Doctor, falling over Gub-Gub in his haste to provide the singer with what she wanted. 'There now, would you mind singing very slowly? Because I want to take down the musical notation and the time is a little complicated. Also, I notice you change the key quite often.' He picked up his pencil. 'All right, I'm ready whenever you are.'

Then the canary began to sing her most beautiful arias. She covered her full range from contralto through mezzo-contralto to her highest soprano notes. The Doctor was amazed.

'How beautiful!' he murmured as he rapidly put the notes on to paper. 'I've never heard anything like it before – in my whole life!'

After about an hour the canary finally stopped. She dipped her beak into the water, raised her head and let it trickle down her throat and said:

'I think that is enough for today. My throat is beginning to get a bit scratchy.'

'Oh, forgive me,' said the Doctor. 'I was so interested – I simply forgot. Please rest – I know that too much vocalizing is bad for your throat.' He closed the notebook and sat back in his chair rubbing his cramped hands.

'You know, Pippinella, for many years now I have wanted to do a series of animal biographies. You're a born story-teller. Would you be willing to help me write your biography?'

'Why, certainly, Doctor,' replied Pippinella. 'When would you like to begin?'

'Any time you feel rested enough,' said the Doctor. 'How about tomorrow night?'

'All right,' said the canary. 'I *am* sort of tired tonight.' And she hopped back up on to her perch, tucked her head under her wing and went to sleep.

THE RESCUE

THE next night the Doctor and his family gathered round the table in the caravan. Pippinella's cage was put in the centre and she began her story.

The canary told them how she had been born in an aviary – a small one where the man who raised canaries gave her special attention because of her unusual voice. It was because of this special talent that she finally acquired a master who bought her and carried her off to a new home; an inn where travellers from all over the world stopped on their way to the seaport to eat and sleep the night.

'I was treated with great respect and admiration by the owner of the inn and his wife and children,' she said. 'And I made many friends there. Everybody stopped to speak to me and listen to my songs – it was very gratifying.'

Pippinella went on to tell the Doctor how she had come to change owners again. It happened on a warm spring day when the innkeeper had hung her cage on a hook high up beside the entrance to the inn.

'A tall, superior sort of gentleman got out of a carriage one day,' said the canary, 'and taking notice of me, said:

' "By Jove! What a marvellous singer! Is it a canary?"

' "Yes, my lord," said the innkeeper, coming forward, "a green canary."

' "I'll buy it from you," said the elegant gentleman. "Buckley, my secretary, will pay you whatever the price is. Have it ready to travel with me in the morning, please."

'I saw the innkeeper's face fall at this. For he was very attached to me and the idea of selling me, even for a big price, evidently did not appeal to him. But this grand person was clearly someone he was afraid to displease by refusing.

' "Very good, my lord," said he in a low voice.

'The gentleman who took me home that day turned out to be a Marquis and I was a present for his wife, Marjorie, the Marchioness. She sent for a servant who produced the most elegant cage you ever saw. It was made of solid silver. It had perches of carved ivory and a swing of mother-of-pearl.' The canary closed her eyes and sat dreaming a moment.

'Well,' she went on, 'after living at the castle for some weeks I began to hear rumours of trouble in the Marquis's mines and mills. His wife wanted him to be kinder to the workers and to keep more of them at their jobs. But he said that with the new machinery he did not need even as many as he had.

'Further, I gathered that in one of the mines the workmen had smashed and wrecked the mine. Then soldiers had been called and the fighting *really* began.

'Thousands of men from the mines stormed the Marquis's castle and drove everyone out of the place. In their hurry to leave no one thought about me. In fact, I didn't really know what was happening until, looking downward from my cage outside the tower window, I saw the leader of the mob raise his hand for silence.

'As the crazy mob grew quiet I strained my ears to catch his words. I heard them. And they almost made my heart stand still. For he was ordering them to bring straw from the stables and oil from the cellars. They were going to set the castle on fire!'

At that point Dab-Dab fluttered down off the chair where she had been sitting during the canary's story.

'Time for supper,' she announced. 'We can hear the rest later.'

'Good!' said Gub-Gub. 'I'm hungry.'

'I don't doubt it,' snapped Dab-Dab. 'You're always hungry.' Turning to the Doctor she asked: 'How about you? I don't think you've had a thing to eat since breakfast.'

'Well,' the Doctor replied reluctantly, 'it's not a very good place to stop a story – just when Pippinella is in such grave danger.'

'I don't listen well when I'm not sitting high,' said Gub-Gub

'Oh, nonsense!' replied the duck. 'She wouldn't be here if anything had happened to her.'

'True – true,' murmured the Doctor. 'Let's have supper and finish the story later.'

After they had eaten supper and Dab-Dab had cleared away the dishes, the Doctor and his family all gathered round the table again to hear the outcome of the burning of the castle.

'Just a minute,' said Gub-Gub. 'My chair's too low. I must get a cushion. I don't listen well when I'm not sitting high.'

'Fussbox!' snorted Dab-Dab.

'Well,' Pippinella began, 'you can imagine how I felt – or rather you can't imagine it. No one could without being in my shoes. I really thought my last hour had come. I watched the crowd below in fascinated horror. I saw groups of men running between the front entrance of the castle and the stable, bearing bales of straw. These they piled against the great oak door, and some more inside the main hall, all along the wooden panelling that ran around the room. Then they brought up from the cellar jugs of oil, cans of oil, barrels of oil.

'For a moment there was a strange awed silence while the match was being put to the straw. It was clear that they all realized the seriousness of the crime they were committing. But as the bonfire flared up, sudden and bright, within the hall, a fiendish roar of delight broke from the ragged crew. And, joining hands in a great ring, they danced a wild jig around the burning home of the man they hated.

'What horses were left in the stables had been taken out and tethered in safety among the trees some distance away. Even the Marquis's dogs, a Russian wolf-hound and a King Charles spaniel, had been rescued and led out before the straw was lit. I alone had been overlooked. After the flame had taken well hold of the great oak doors and fire and smoke barred all admittance, some of the men at last caught sight of me, high up on the tower wall. For I saw several pointing up. But if they had wanted to save me then it was too late. The panelling, the doors, the floors, the stairs, everything of wood in the lower part of the building was now a seething, roaring mass of flame.

'Waves of hot air, clouds of choking smoke, flurries of burning sparks swirled upward around my silver cage. The smoke was the worst. At first I thought I would surely be suffocated long before I was burned.

'But luckily, soon after the fire started, a fitful breeze began. And every once in a while, when I thought I had reached my last gasp, the wind would sweep the rising smoke away to the side and give me a chance to breathe again.

'From my position I could see inside the tower through the open window, as well as down on to the woods and all around outside. And presently, as I peered into the room, wondering if any help could come from that quarter, I saw a mouse run out into the middle of the floor in a great state of excitement.

' "Where's the smoke coming from?" she cried. 'What's burning?"

' "The castle's on fire," I said. 'Come up here and see if you can gnaw a hole through this cage of mine. I'm going to be roasted if somebody doesn't let me out."

' "What do you think I am?" she said – "a pair of pliers or a file? I can't eat through silver. Besides, I've got a family of five children down in my hole under the floor. I must look after them."

'She ran to the door, muttering to herself, and disappeared down the winding stair. In a minute she was back again.

' "I can't take them that way,' she said. "Below the third landing the whole staircase is burning."

'She sprang up on to the window-sill. It's funny how little details, in moments of great distress, stick in your mind. I remember.exactly how she looked, not six inches from the wall of my cage, this tiny creature gazing over the lip of the stone window-sill, down from that tremendous height into the garden and the tree-tops far below. Her whiskers trembled and her nose twitched at the end. She wasn't concerned about me, shut up and powerless to escape – though goodness knows she had stolen my food often enough. All she was thinking of was those wretched little brats of hers in the nest beneath the floor.

' "Bother it!" the mouse muttered. "What a distance. Well, it's the only chance. I might as well begin."

'And she turned around, sprang down into the room, shot across the floor and disappeared into her hole. She wasn't gone more than a moment. When she showed up again she had a scrubby little pink baby in her mouth, without any fur on it yet and eyes still closed. It looked like a pig the size of a bean. She came to the edge of the sill and without the least hesitation started out on the face of the wall, scrambling her way along the mortar cracks between the stones. You'd think it would be impossible even for a mouse to make its way down the outside

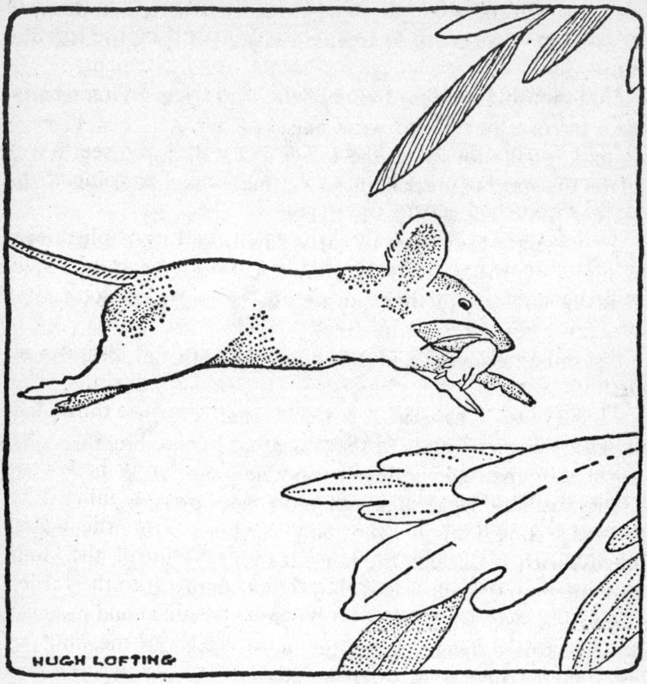

'Still clutching her scrubby youngster in her teeth, she leapt!'

of a high tower like that. But the weather and rain had worn the joints deep in most places; and they have a wonderful way of clinging, have mice.

'I watched her get two thirds of the way down, and then the heat and smoke of the fire below were too much for her. I saw her looking across at the tree, whose top-most boughs came close to the tower. She measured the distance with her eye. And, still clutching her scrubby youngster in her teeth, she leapt. She just caught the end-most leaves with her claws. And the slender limb swayed gently downward with her weight.

Then she scuttled along the bough, reached the trunk, dumped her child in some crack or crevice and started back to fetch the rest.

'That mouse, to get her five children singly over that long trip, had a terrible lot of hard work ahead of her. As I watched her scrambling laboriously up the tower again, disappearing in and out of the mortar cracks, an idea came to me. And when she regained the window-sill I said to her:

' "You've got four more to carry down. And the fire is creeping higher up the stairs every minute. If I was out of my cage I could fly down with them in a tenth of the time you'd take. Why don't you try to set me free?"

'I saw her glance up at me shrewdly with her little beady eyes.

' "I don't trust canaries," she said after a moment. 'And in any case there's no place in that cage that I could bite through."

'And she ran off to her hole for another load.

'She was back even quicker than the first time.

" 'It's getting hot under the floor," she said. "And the smoke is already drifting through the joints. I think I'll bring all the children out on to the sill, so that they won't suffocate."

'And she went and fetched the remainder of her precious family and laid them side by side on the stone beside my cage. Then, taking one at a time, she started off to carry them to safety. Four times I saw her descend that giddy zigzag trail of hers into the welter of smoke and sparks that seethed, denser and blacker every minute, about the base of the tower. And four more times she made that leap from the sheer face of the stonework, with a baby in her mouth, across the tips of the tree boughs. The leaves of these were now blackened and scorched with the high-reaching fire. On the third trip I saw that mouse actually jump through tongues of flames. But still she came back for the fourth. As she reached the sill for the last load she was staggering and weak and I could see that her fur and whiskers had been singed.

'It was not many minutes after she had gone for good that I heard a tremendous crash inside the tower and a shower of sparks came up into the little round room. The long spiral staircase, or part of it, had fallen down. Its lower supports had been burnt away below. I sometimes think that that was the thing that saved me as much as anything else. Because it cut off my little room at the top from the burning woodwork lower down. If the fire had ever reached that room I would have been gone for sure. For, although my cage was in the open air outside, it was much too close to the edge of the window to be safe. Below me I could now see flames pouring out of the windows, just as though they were furnace chimneys.

'I saw the leader of the workmen shout to his men to keep well back from the walls. They evidently expected the whole tower soon to crumble and fall down. That would mean the end for me, of course, because I would almost certainly fall right into the middle of the fire raging on the lower floors.

'In answer to their leader's orders the men were moving off among the trees, when I noticed that some new excitement had caught their attention. They began talking and calling to one another and pointing down the hill towards the foot of the woods. Then, gathering up what stolen goods they could carry, they scattered away from the castle, looking backward over their shoulders towards the woods as they ran. In two minutes there wasn't one of them left in sight. The mouse had gone. The men had gone. I was alone with the fire.

'And then suddenly, in a lull in the roaring of the flames, I heard a sound that brought hope back into my despairing heart. It was the rap-rap-rap, rap-a-tap, tap of a drum.

'I sprang to my perch and craned my neck to look out over the woods. And there, winding towards me, up the road, far, far off, like a thin red ribbon, were soldiers marching in fours!

'By the time the soldiers reached the castle the smoke coming up from below was so bad that I could see only occasionally with any clearness at all. I was now gasping and choking for breath and felt very dizzy in the head. I managed to make out, however, that the officer in charge was dividing his men into two parties. One, which he took command of himself, went off in pursuit of the workmen. The other was left behind to put out the fire. But the castle, of course, was entirely ruined. Shortly after they arrived one of the side walls of the main hall fell in with a crash and a large part of the room came down with it. Yet my tower still stood.

'There was a large fish-pond not far from the front door. And the soldiers got a lot of buckets from the stables and formed a chain, handing the water up to some of their companions, who threw it on the fire.

'Almost immediately the heat and smoke rising around my cage began to lessen. But, of course, it took hours of this bucket work to get the fire really under control.

'The officer with the other party returned. Seeing there was nothing more he could do, he now left a sergeant in charge and taking one of the soldiers with him, went back down the road leading through the woods. The rest continued with the work of fighting the fire and making sure that it did not break out again.

'As soon as my ears had caught the cheerful beating of that drum I had started singing. But on account of the smoke my song had been little more than coughs and splutters. Now, however, with the air cleared, I opened my throat and let go for all I was worth, *Maids, come out, the coach is here*. And the old sergeant, who was superintending the soldiers' work, lifted his head and listened. He couldn't make out where the sound was coming from. But presently he caught sight of my cage, way up at the top of the blackened tower.

' "By Jove, boys!" I heard him cry. "A canary! The sole survivor of the garrison. Let's get him for good luck."

'But getting me was no easy matter. Piles of fallen stonework now covered every entrance. Then they searched the stables for a ladder. They found one long enough to reach the lowest of the tower windows. But the soldier who scaled it called down to his companions that the staircase inside was gone and he could get no higher. Nevertheless, the old sergeant was determined to get me.

'The sergeant was convinced that I, who had come through such a fire and could still sing songs, would bring luck to any regiment. And he swore a tremendous oath that he would get me down or break his neck. Then he went back to the stable and got some ropes and himself ascended the ladder to the bottom window of the tower. By throwing the rope over broken beams and other bits of ruined woodwork that still remained within, he hauled himself upward little by little. And finally I saw his funny face appear through the hole in the floor of my room where the staircase had been. He had a terrible scar across his cheek, from an old wound, I suppose. But it was a nice face, for all that.

'"Hulloa, my lad!" said he, hoisting himself into the room and coming to the window. "So you're the only one who stood by the castle, eh? By the hinges of hell, you're a real soldier, you are! You come and join the Fusiliers, Dick. And we'll make you the mascot of the regiment."

'As my rescuer stuck his head out of the window to lift my cage off its nail his companions down below sent up a cheer. He fastened his rope to the silver ring of the cage and started to lower me down the outside of the tower. I descended slowly, swinging like the pendulum of some great clock from that enormous height. And finally I landed safe on solid earth in the midst of a crowd of cheering soldiers.

'And that is how another chapter in my life ended – and still another began.'

DOCTOR DOLITTLE
and
THE SECRET LAKE
ILLUSTRATED BY THE AUTHOR
BY HUGH LOFTING

MUDFACE, THE TURTLE

AMONG the Doctor's old friends was an ancient turtle by the name of Mudface. He lived in Lake Junganyika. So long had he lived that when Noah built the Ark he was only a young turtle and – being a water creature – had lived through the great Flood that covered the whole earth.

On one of the Doctor's voyages many years ago he had visited Mudface. Finding him suffering with rheumatism from the dampness – and old age – John Dolittle had persuaded millions of birds to bring pebbles and sand and drop them into the lake to build an island for the turtle. In this way Mudface could bask in the sunlight – which seemed to help his rheumatism.

One day Cheapside and Becky, his wife, the London sparrows, arrived at the Doctor's house in Puddleby-on-the-Marsh, breathless and gasping from exhaustion. They had flown to and from Africa.

'Cheapside,' the Doctor scolded, 'I never heard of anything so utterly crazy! Just the two of you to make such a trip! Four thousand miles. I never intended, when I asked you to inquire about Mudface, that you should go *yourself*.'

'Quite right, Doc,' murmured the sparrow.

'Why, you could have run into an equinoctial gale at this time of the year,' said the Doctor.

'Jim-in-ey, Doc!' gasped Cheapside. 'You never saw such a wind! Nearly blew us inside out.'

Then Becky broke in impatiently.

'For pity's sake, Cheapside,' she scolded. 'Tell the Doctor what we found. You can tell him how you suffered later.'

John Dolittle nodded.

'All right, all right!' said the sparrow impatiently. 'You'd

'Cheapside,' the Doctor scolded

never know the ol' place. They 'ad a big shake-up – sort of a earthquake. Some friends of ours – wild ducks, they was – said poor old Muddyface got hisself buried when the quake busted his island in two.'

'Good heavens!' the Doctor murmured.

Cheapside had many more details to tell the Doctor but, after hearing the sparrow out, we began hasty plans for rescuing the old turtle.

A few weeks later, paddling down the Little Fantippo River towards Lake Junganyika, the Doctor said to me:

'Stubbins, our best bet is to find my old friend Jim.'

'You mean the crocodile? I asked.

'Yes,' replied the Doctor. 'The same fellow who lived with us. You remember, Sarah accused him of eating the linoleum.'

Well, it didn't take us long to find Jim. He was well known by all the crocodiles in Africa. They sent word from river to river that John Dolittle was looking for him and in no time he came up beside our canoe.

'Here comes your friend Jim to welcome you, Doc,' cried Cheapside. 'Good old Jim!'

It was a great and important meeting; and when Jim lifted his head out of the water many questions were asked and answered. Myself, I could only understand, so far, a few words of the language.

Once or twice the Doctor explained to me what was being said. But, as he was in great haste, he asked Jim to turn around and swim beside our canoe as we went on upstream. It seemed the messenger who sent word for Jim to meet the Doctor had also told him to bring some crocodiles along to assist in the finding of Mudface.

In the books of the life of Doctor Dolittle there are a few places where I have written of certain happenings which I shall never be able to forget: scenes that are pictured so lastingly in my memory that today, years afterwards, I can see them all over again, exactly as they took place. And this, as we paddled up close to the trail-landing of the Great South Bend, was one of those pictures that was to stay in my memory for life, clear and unforgettable.

The right bank of the river rose here to quite a height. And down this slope the great beasts from the Niger were pouring – in a solid procession – into the Little Fantippo River. The jungle, whose heavy tangle covered all the land on either bank, had here been torn up and cleaned off by millions of clawed feet, making a wide, crowded road.

You could barely see the ground they walked on – only the creatures' backs, as close as stitches in a carpet. But once in a while a free spot in the parade would open up; and then you saw that the earth had been trodden as smooth as a pavement.

As they reached the water's edge, this great army did not stop or hesitate a moment. They flopped into the river a hundred abreast and headed upstream.

Old Jim now left us and swam out to a low flat rock in mid-stream. On to this he crawled and began directing the traffic – exactly like a policeman at a busy street-crossing.

I glanced up the river and saw that this seemed to have changed into a solid mass of reptiles. Dry-shod you could have walked from bank to bank on their backs. After about another half hour John Dolittle sent Polynesia over to the rock with a message for Jim.

And Jim began swinging his tail wildly from side to side. Clearly the Doctor's message was: 'Enough!' For very soon I could see the swarm of crocodiles pouring over the trail begin to thin out – to grow less crowded. I suppose Jim's message was sent back from mouth to mouth all the way to the Niger River.

As the light was now fading fast the Doctor was anxious to pitch camp. A place was found, this time on the left bank. As soon as we had the hammocks set up and a nice fire burning, the Doctor had a talk with Jim. This time either John Dolittle or Chee-Chee translated everything for me.

I had been anxious to get a good, close-up look at this famous reptile who had, quite unintentionally, so upset the Doctor's household years ago on account of Sarah, the Doctor's sister. Well, it may be hard for you to imagine a crocodile looking friendly and quite un-dangerous, but this one did.

The Doctor's own animals all knew Jim, of course; and none was in the least afraid of him. Not even the white mouse was scared – indeed, he kept running up and down the great beast's knobbly back, from nose to tail. Whitey's only worry was that he might miss something that was being said. And he never seemed to be certain whether it was Jim's head or Jim's tail that was doing the talking.

I could not help thinking that if any of the good people of Puddleby were to come upon us now and see John Dolittle, M.D., sitting over a fire in the African jungle and talking with a crocodile, his reputation as a crazy man would surely be more firmly fixed on him than ever.

Jim told the Doctor that he had already been up to the Secret Lake. He had taken two of his brothers with him. They had gone all around the island to make sure where the turtle had disappeared.

'I am very hopeful, Doctor,' said he, 'from what we saw of the lake bottom at the north end of the island, that we shall be able to dig your friend out all right. Only it may take us a couple of days, possibly longer.'

'How far,' asked the Doctor, 'do you calculate we are from the Secret Lake now?'

'Not a great distance,' said the crocodile. 'I think we should easily reach it tomorrow afternoon.'

By this time our supper had been prepared and eaten. And so, with the comforting picture of our journey's end at last so near, we turned in and went to sleep.

GENERAL JIM

At daybreak we were up and paddling towards the lake. In the mist we could see very little but soon the sun cleared the fog and we finally came in sight of Mudface's island.

I had had no idea how large it was. And it was hard to believe that birds alone had built this body of land, stone by stone.

Now, as we stopped in the shadow of it – our long journey ended at last – I gazed at it with curiosity and respect. Here, John Dolittle had, through his friendship with the Animal Kingdom, actually changed geography in a small way.

Kneeling up in the canoe, I could see, everywhere I looked, little beady eyes of the crocodiles, who had now all crawled ashore and resting in the undergrowth. The water was very still and clear and calm.

A sudden splash made me turn my head. The Doctor had taken off his clothes and dived overboard. For a moment I thought he was going to swim right down to the turtle. But in a moment he bobbed up again and said:

'Stubbins, you'll find a short coil of rope – underneath the grub-box, I think. Get it out and tie it in a loop for me, will you? Jim's brother is going to tow me down to Mudface.'

In a moment I got the rope, tied the loop, and handed one end to Jim's brother. John Dolittle grabbed the other end and his tow-horse plunged downward under water. As they disappeared I noted the exact time on my watch. Jim stayed close by to go after the Doctor should he stay down longer than I thought safe.

One minute and ten seconds – the tiny hand went jumping round the dial . . . One minute and twenty seconds . . . One minute and twenty-five seconds – my right arm rose straight up to give Jim the signal I had arranged. And then suddenly there was a swirl of water at the canoe's other end. The Doctor's head appeared. He was gasping for breath. He still had hold of the towing rope. But now there were three or four crocodiles around him who seemed to be bearing him up. However, I could tell at once that he was all right, even if badly exhausted.

Polynesia called to me to come forward and make the rope fast, so that if the Doctor went unconscious he could not slip under water. Then the crocodile nosed the canoe to the shore of the island. This took only a few minutes. And soon we had the canoe alongside a gravel landing where we could unload. I spread a tarpaulin and got John Dolittle to lie down and rest; meanwhile Chee-Chee slung a hammock and Jip scurried around and collected wood for a fire.

Presently (looking like a Red Indian chief in the blanket which I had got out of the baggage for him), John Dolittle crouched over a cheerful blaze. Polynesia, Cheapside and I waited for him till he should have breath enough to speak.

At last, with a deep sigh, he straightened his shoulders, then turned and looked at me, smiling.

'By George, Stubbins!' said he in a low voice. 'Kind of – kind of out of training – for that sort of thing . . . My goodness, I'm winded!'

'It's not surprising, Doctor,' I answered. 'You gave me a real scare. One minute and thirty-one seconds.'

'Hah, good old Stubbins!' he puffed. 'So you kept track of me with the watch, eh? What *would* I do without you?'

'How did you find things, Doctor? Is the turtle still alive?'

'I'm pretty sure he is,' said John Dolittle. 'It's hard to tell, though. We can't wake him up. He's fast asleep.'

'*Asleep!*' I cried. 'I don't understand.'

'Conditions,' said the Doctor. 'Just hibernation conditions. The earthquake which buried Mudface came at the exact month of the year which is the regular time for turtles to start their hibernation – their winter sleep.'

There was a moment's silence. It was broken by Cheapside, who had been listening thoughtfully.

'Asleep, is 'e? Well, swamp me pink, Doc! After we makes a record trip to rescue 'im, we finds the old boy takin' 'is after-dinner nap! – Criminy! That's what I'll do next time Becky starts one of 'er lectures on the duties of a good father. "hush my dear!" I'll say. "I feel my 'ibernation comin' on." ' (Cheapside closed his eyes, sighing noisily.) ' "*Sh!* Can't you see I'm gettin' drowsy? 'Bye, 'bye! You may call me in April – if the weather's good." '

The three crocodiles had already gathered all the other leaders and heads of families to listen to the Doctor's instructions. And a strange looking council of war they made, crowded around Big Chief Dolittle (still wrapped in his red blanket).

'Listen, Jim,' said the Doctor, 'now that you have cleared the gravel off the *top* of the turtle, why not set a big gang to work prying *under* his lower shell?'

'I understand, Doctor,' said Jim. 'You want us to let the water leak in under him at one place to break the mud suction?'

'That's it exactly,' said the Doctor. 'But for pity's sake be careful you don't crack his shell. You had better pry him up by the shoulder – a turtle's lower shell is thicker there.'

'All right,' said Jim.

As soon as the Doctor had spoken, Jim gave out orders to all the leaders. Then many things seemed to start happening at

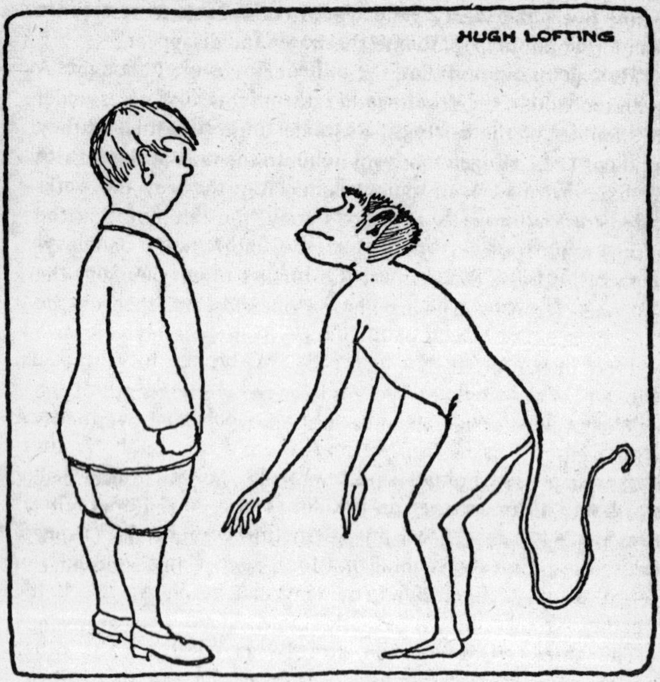

Even with Chee-Chee's help as a translator, I couldn't keep track of it all

once. Even with Chee-Chee's help as a translator, I couldn't keep track of it all. But later on I managed to put things together and write them into my notebook.

First of all, a strange noise struck my ear. This was the *plop, plop – splash, splash,* as all those great beasts, in sixes and sevens, threw themselves off the land into the lake. The leaders had been ordered by Jim to divide the diggers into regular work-teams. As the Doctor had told me, it was very exhausting. So, as soon as one lot was tired out, the order would be given to change over; the weary gang would come back to rest and a fresh lot would *plop, plop* into the water and disappear.

The way they went about it was very clever, I thought. A dozen crocodiles, set close together, thrust their flat noses under the shoulder of the turtle's shell, as deep into the mud as they could go. Then a dozen more got up on to the tails of the first lot and bore down with all their weight. From the way the water started to flow in under Mudface's body, Jim felt sure that the suction must soon let go. He got two more gangs of heavy-weights and lined them up on the turtle's other shoulder, the right one. Then, by heaving first on one side and then on the other, he got the whole of Mudface's front part levered up a good foot out of the mud.

At last, as the water rushed in under the whole length of the turtle from head to tail, the great beast's body rolled over on its back, free!

I cannot say what picture as to Mudface's size I had ever had. Cheapside had spoken of him airily, 'as big as a house' – but I knew the sparrow often exaggerated. I had heard the Doctor tell of the turtle's size as 'unbelievably large' or 'perfectly huge' – which could mean anything.

But when at last I saw him with my own eyes – though really I only saw part of him that night – I thought I must be having a nightmare.

Twilight was coming on now. But you could still see pretty well – except where the setting sun threw the island's long shadow on the calm water. John Dolittle was standing on the shore staring out into the wide and silent Junganyika.

Presently, in this darker shaded part of the lake, I thought I saw something come to the surface, gently breaking the calm of the water – something round and flat, like a ball just afloat. At first it seemed no bigger than a tea-tray. But as it rose, it slowly grew – larger and larger and larger still.

Close behind me I heard the Doctor give a long sigh of relief.

'Thank goodness! . . . They've managed it . . . Here he comes!'

Too-Too, the night-seer, made some clicking noises with his

tongue, while Chee-Chee, always so brave in real danger, whimpered fearfully somewhere in the gloom.

I could tell that this great mass out there had stopped rising and was slowly moving towards us. And, from the smoothness of its motion, I guessed it must be swimming.

'Well, well, the lucky voyage, Stubbins!' the Doctor whispered over my shoulder. 'The lucky voyage!'

John Dolittle was never one to make a show of his feelings. (This, Polynesia had often said, was the most English thing about him.) But as the strong fingers of his right hand suddenly gripped my shoulder, they told me, better than any words, how much this successful ending to our voyage meant for him.

Exactly when I first saw the turtle's head I don't know. My eyes were busy staring down into the water, watching for what might come out of it. There was a single large palm tree quite close to me. I had noticed Chee-Chee the monkey look up at the top of this palm from time to time; and I suppose my own gaze followed his. Anyway, I saw something else, swaying against the sky. It was the same height as the top of the tree. I suddenly knew what it was. *It was Mudface's head!*

And, in the way we often get reminded in great moments of things unimportant and far away, I thought of the picture in the Doctor's library back home. It showed big lizards who roamed the earth thousands of years ago, nibbling the leaves from the tops of the forest.

But my dreaming thoughts were suddenly brought back. The ground beneath my feet seemed to be trembling. Was this another earthquake, I wondered? . . . No. This monster, towering over us, was *speaking* to the Doctor.

How thrilled I was to find I could understand what this thunderous voice was saying! Later, when I was writing out his story of the Flood, I was to miss a word or sentence here and there; and I had to fill them in later. But this evening, when Mudface spoke his greeting to his old friend, I caught every word of it – perfectly. I felt very proud, I can tell you, as I wrote down the great animal's first rumbling words in my notebook:

'Again, John Dolittle, you come in time of danger, in time of trouble – as you have always done. For this, the creatures of the land, the water and the air shall remember your name when other men, called *great*, shall be forgotten. Welcome, good friend! – Welcome once more to Lake Junganyika.'

DOCTOR DOLITTLE'S PUDDLEBY ADVENTURES

WRITTEN & ILLUSTRATED BY HUGH LOFTING

THE DOG AMBULANCE

IT was about this time that the Dog Ambulance was started. This institution (the idea, you may remember, was originally Jip's) belonged to and was organized entirely by the Club. It was the first thing of its kind in history. And I felt that a description of it and the events that accompanied its inauguration could quite fittingly be included in my book, *Tales of the Home for Cross-bred Dogs*. On consulting Jip, I found that he agreed with me and we decided to put it in following the Dalmatian's story.

For several days in succession we had had serious cases of dog casualties on the streets: dogs run over; dogs kicked by horses; sick and homeless strays, etc. Many of these cases when brought to the surgery were so far gone that the Doctor had a hard time pulling them through.

'Tommy,' said Jip, coming to me at breakfast one morning, 'we've got to have a Dog Ambulance. I'm sure we can get the Doctor to agree to it because I've already spoken to him about it – the time we brought Kling here when he was poisoned – and he thought it was a good idea. In the Home we have a couple of mongrel greyhounds. They're kind of funny to look at, but they're awful speedy. They have already volunteered to take it in turns doing duty. So we will have no difficulty with that part of it. What we need is the ambulance carriage itself and some harness for the greyhounds. Do you think you could build us a carriage and get your father to make us a set of harness?'

'Well, Jip,' I said, 'I don't know. But I am quite willing to try.'

So that same evening I went over to the Stubbins' cobbler shop where I found that my father, though he was pretty busy, would make us the harness in his spare time. Then I set to work

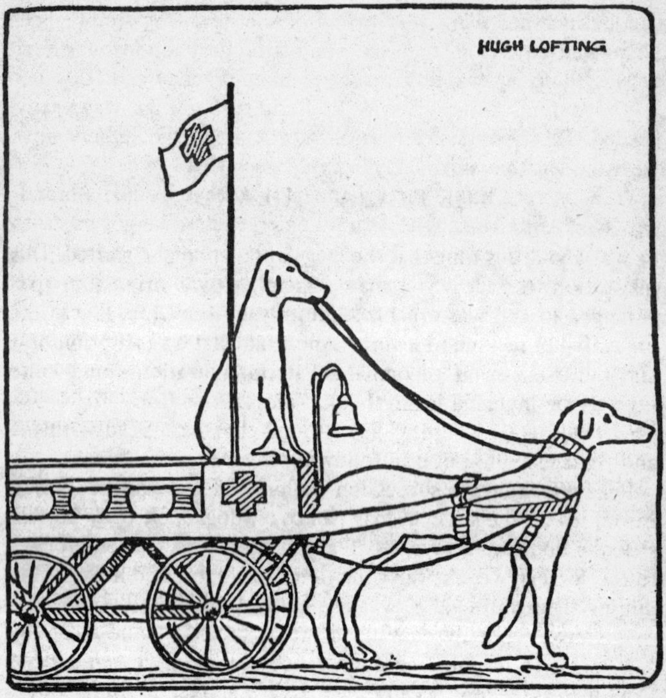

It was quite an elegant turnout

and, out of a pair of rubber-tyred perambulator wheels, a few springs out of an old bed and some pieces of packing-case, we constructed a very decent-looking runabout, light enough to be drawn by a dog. We painted it white, put a red-cross flag on it and a bell. It was quite an elegant turnout.

When the harness was ready we hitched up one of the mongrel greyhounds, and Jip, as assistant casualty surgeon, drove around the zoo enclosure at a speed of thirty miles an hour – greatly to the astonishment of the inhabitants of Animal Town.

All concerned were very proud of the new Dog Ambulance. Night and day, from then on, one of the greyhounds was kept harnessed up in readiness to answer an emergency call.

'That's fine, Tommy,' said Jip, 'something that was really needed. Those serious cases can be brought to the surgery now with the least possible delay.'

Well, as such things often happen, now that we had a brand-new Dog Ambulance ready for all emergencies, we got no cases to try it out. Suddenly all dog casualties seemed to cease. The gallant greyhound steeds stood in the harness from dawn to dark and never a call came for their services.

Jip, Kling and Toby, the chief organizers of the Animal Town First Aid, were dreadfully disappointed. Finally Jip became so anxious to try out the new ambulance that he and Toby decided secretly between them that if no case came along soon they would have to make one.

After many days of idle waiting they had (without telling either the Doctor or me) proudly led their ambulance out through the streets of Puddleby on their own. This they did partly because they wanted the townsfolk to see the elegant equipage in all its glory, and partly because they might find a 'case' by chance to try it on.

While they were parading through the town they came upon Gub-Gub, the Doctor's pet pig, in a back street sitting on a garbage heap. He was a great garbage-heap explorer, was Gub-Gub. The poor pig had eaten some bad turnips and was looking rather green in the face from a slight stomach-ache.

'Ah! A serious case!' cried Jip, rushing the ambulance up alongside the garbage heap in grand style. Then with great dispatch Orderlies Kling and Toby, under the direction of Surgeon Jip, pounced upon the wretched Gub-Gub and began hauling him on to the ambulance. They would have sooner had a dog patient to try their new equipment on, but a pig was better than nothing.

'Leave me alone!' bawled Gub-Gub, kicking out in all directions. 'I've only got a stomach-ache. I don't want to go on your ambulance!'

He was a great garbage-heap explorer

'Don't listen to him,' ordered Jip. 'He's delirious. Appendicitis most likely. It's a rush case, men. Get him on quick!'

The three of them rolled Gub-Gub's portly carcass on to the ambulance. Jip sprang into the driver's seat while Toby and Kling sat on the 'delirious' patient to hold him down.

Like a shot out of a gun the mongrel greyhound bounded away at full speed for the Doctor's home. Meanwhile Jip clanged the bell for all he was worth to clear the road ahead and drown the bellowings of the first case to be brought to the Dolittle surgery by the Dog Ambulance.

THE MISHAP AT KINGSBRIDGE

IT was a thrilling ride – thrilling for the staff of the ambulance, for the townsfolk who looked on, and most of all for the patient. Certainly all records established up to that date were easily broken so far as sheer speed was concerned. But as to time – from picking up a case to delivery at hospital – that was another matter. Indeed, the original case never reached the surgery at all – in the ambulance. But I must tell the story in the proper order.

Streaking up the High Street with clanging bell, the strange vehicle shot under horses' noses, past traffic policemen who ordered it to stop, round corners on two wheels, scattering scared pedestrians right and left. At Kingsbridge it met with its first accident. Here the road narrowed as it crossed the river. In trying to avoid a peddler's barrow the greyhound steed went a shade too near a lamp-post. With Gub-Gub's extra heavy weight added to that of the two orderlies and the surgeon, the springs of the ambulance were being taxed to their utmost anyway. The hub of the right rear wheel only just touched the base of the lamp-post. But it was enough to throw the overloaded, careening carriage off its balance. On one wheel it shot across the road and dumped its entire contents, surgeon, orderlies and patient, over the parapet of the bridge.

As it happened, the river was at low tide. At such times, wide stretches of black mud margined the narrow, swiftly running stream. This in a way was providential – for the patient, but not for the staff. Gub-Gub's rating as a swimmer was very low, and had the river been at high tide he would have had a hard time reaching the bank. Jip, Kling and Toby, on the other hand, would have much preferred a clean bath to the fate that awaited them below the bridge. All four landed with an oozy splash into the tidal mud. It broke the fall nicely but it didn't improve their appearance. Entirely black from head to foot, the gallant staff still remembered its duty to the injured and proceeded to dig the struggling, squealing patient out of his mud bath.

Fortunately, the distance to firmer ground was not more than a few yards. Somehow the patient, who on account of his weight had sunk deeper in than the others, was hauled and dragged to solid territory. He may not have been a proper case for the ambulance when they had forcibly carried him off from the garbage heap, but by the time they had got him out of the mud of the river he was in considerably greater need of attention.

Regaining the bridge, the staff, now completely garbed in a new uniform of black mud, rolled the patient back on to the ambulance, jumped in after him and went away as fast as ever. In fact, they went even faster, for their mishap at the river had caused quite a crowd to collect and they were afraid they might be stopped at any minute.

For about a mile all went well. But as they turned into the Oxenthorpe Road at full gallop they met with still another accident. A sleek, overfed Pomeranian was crossing the road with great dignity. Suddenly, seeing the extraordinary carriage bearing down upon him at thirty-five miles an hour, he lost the little wits he had, ran first this way and then that and finally wound up under the front wheels of the ambulance. The carriage did not entirely capsize, but it tipped up sufficiently as it went over him to shoot the patient out again – this time into the gutter. The fiery greyhound steed was brought to a standstill and that keen – perhaps too keen – medical student, Jip, ran back to take charge of the situation.

The patient was lying on his back in the gutter, his four trotters waving in the air, yelling blue murder. Up the middle of the road the fat Pomeranian was also lying on his back and howling – mostly with indignation and fright. Surgeon Jip and Orderlies Toby and Kling held a hasty professional consultation. The ambulance could hardly take both casualties. The first duty was their original patient. On the other hand, the Dog Ambulance was originally intended for dogs, and here was a fine case ready at hand.

However, while the discussion was still going on, Gub-Gub, fearing he might have to continue his hazardous ride in the ambulance, suddenly sprang up and took to his heels. Sore as he was from his fall and his stomache-ache, he had had enough of Jip's first aid.

This solved the problem for the staff of the Dog Ambulance very nicely. Jip grabbed the Pomeranian by the scruff of the neck and, carrying him like a puppy, dumped him into the ambulance, sprang in once more and gave the word to go.

It wasn't until after the flying carriage had done another mile that he suddenly realized that he had left his two orderlies behind. But Kling and Toby, by putting on their best speed, came in on foot a very good second and third in the race for the surgery.

THE RECEPTION AT THE SURGERY

JIP Kling and Toby were all sadly disappointed at the Doctor's reception of the Dog Ambulance for the first time it returned from active service. I am bound to say that the equipment had lost much of its original smartness. The wheels were bent and wobbly, the bell post was twisted up like a corkscrew and the bell gone, the first-aid box beneath the driver's seat had burst open and bandages were trailing from it in the dust of the road behind. As for the staff, caked with mud and dust from head to foot, well, you could just tell that they were dogs and that was all.

The patient, as soon as the ambulance came to a halt, got out of the stretcher without waiting for assistance and at once began a long and indignant speech to the Doctor. He accused Jip and his assistants of first knocking him down by reckless driving, and then kidnapping him right in front of his own gate.

No sooner had he finished his tirade than his mistress, who had followed in a cab, appeared upon the scene and began another long accusation. She assured the Doctor that she had heard a good deal about him and his crazy wild animals and she meant to appeal to the police. Things had come to a pretty pass, she said, when a man trained a gang of dogs to kidnap and steal other dogs.

The Doctor was just getting ready to answer her when Gub-Gub arrived, howling like a lost child who had been punished for something he never did. He began the third discourse upon the wicked deeds of the Red Cross Brigade who had carried him off against his will, thrown him over a bridge into the river, then rushed him over bumpy streets a few more miles and finally pitched him out into the gutter.

By the end of the last of these speeches the staff of the Dog Ambulance was beginning to feel that its services in the public good had been somewhat misdirected and not wholly understood. The greyhound steed slunk away to the zoo enclosure, where I undid his harness and separated him from the dilapidated carriage. As for Jip, Kling and Toby, they made no attempt to explain to the Doctor, but went miserably down to the fish-pond and washed the mud from themselves. Not a word was said till they were on their way back to supper. Then Jip broke the silence with, 'We shouldn't have started with that ridiculous pig. He always puts a hoodoo on everything.'

THE DOLITTLE BOOKS

THE STORY OF DR DOLITTLE. 'A work of genius. It is the first real children's classic since *Alice*.' *Hugh Walpole*

THE VOYAGES OF DR DOLITTLE. 'Children will delight in this book. *Dr Dolittle* wins all hearts.' *The Times Literary Supplement*

DR DOLITTLE'S POST OFFICE. 'Incomparably the best new book for children of the year.' *Spectator*

DR DOLITTLE'S CIRCUS. 'The purest delight ... as good as the rest of the books dealing with that immortal and delightful person.' *Observer*

DR DOLITTLE'S ZOO. 'It is with genuine regret that we once more say good-bye to the little man who manages to combine Franciscan heroism and charm with homely sanity.' *Nation*

DR DOLITTLE'S CARAVAN. 'A lively and ingenious "Dolittle", and although at the end of the book he has retired to Pubbleby, we cannot believe that he is anywhere near the end of his activities.' *The Times Literary Supplement*

DR DOLITTLE'S GARDEN. 'No books of our time can compare with these for communicating to youthful readers those constant glows of appreciation that make them gurgle with joy.' *Daily Telegraph*

DR DOLITTLE IN THE MOON. 'Each generation cries for the moon in turn, and the very newest one will find in these pages not something to cry for, but something to completely satisfy their fleeting fancy.' *Spectator*

DR DOLITTLE'S RETURN. 'It is, indeed, good news that this most lovable man has returned from the moon.' *Lady Cynthia Asquith* in the *Daily Telegraph*

DR DOLITTLE AND THE SECRET LAKE. 'Humorous, eventful, and never condescending in tone.' *Irish Times*

DR DOLITTLE AND THE GREEN CANARY. 'Dr Dolittle long ago joined the small band of those chosen by children as worthy of more than casual notice.' *Manchester Guardian*

DR DOLITTLE'S PUDDLEBY ADVENTURES. 'Hugh Lofting will take his place among the immortal humorists who have given pleasure to countless millions of readers.' *Children's Newspaper*

Hello, I'm FAT PUFFIN
Would YOU like to find out more about Puffin books and authors, enter competitions and get a chance to buy new books?
Then join The Puffin Club!
Puffin Post
You will get a copy of the Club magazine four times a year, a membership book and a badge.
And there's lots more! For further details and an application form send a stamped, addressed envelope to:
The Puffin Club Dept. A
Penguin Books Ltd.,
Bath Road,
Harmondsworth,
Middlesex UB7 ODA
If you live in AUSTRALIA write to: The Australian Puffin Club, Penguin Books Australia Ltd., P.O. Box 257, Ringwood, Victoria 3134